Nineteen Unsaid

Alice Cox

Dedication

I dedicate this book to anyone who has had to learn to survive sexual trauma. The broken reflection you see in the mirror is far from the real you. I pray my story in some way helps you to not feel alone in your journey of healing.

I also dedicate this book to my mother for seeing me when I could no longer see myself. She is truly my angel.

Contents

Oh nineteen. How is it that over ten years have come and gone, and I still remember every moment of that year as if it were yesterday? I have these moments, especially now as a mother, where I feel so completely free of it all, and other moments or even days that suck me right back in. Especially when October comes around; October through January, my mind still takes me back. The smell of a bonfire, Halloween, my birthday, seeing or hearing from old friends, watching certain movies...it brings me back to the melancholy essence of that year of my life. It was one of the craziest emotional roller coasters I've ever experienced, and that's putting it lightly. But at the beginning of it, I remember nothing but a transcendent feeling of pure happiness. Outside of falling in love with my husband and having children, the months surrounding turning nineteen were probably the happiest I've ever been in my life. I was free…for a little while anyway.

January 10th, 2013, changed my life forever. There's not a day that goes by that I don't think about it in one way or another. Sometimes I experience a reflection of gratitude for finally feeling beyond it. Other times, the past can feel like an all-consuming clenching of my breath as I remember laying in the backseat of a truck as my "best friend" raped me. That night is always there, tucked into the shadows of my mind, and I still involuntarily relive it. However, I no longer give the horrific remembrance power over my heart the way I once did. I have learned over the years that while that scar will never go away, the darkness of the memory does not hold me prisoner anymore; *it does not define me*. It took me nearly ten years, but through an unfortunate series of events, I miraculously found myself again. I guess that makes those events not so unfortunate because they helped shape who I am today. This is not a story unlike many others out there; frankly, it is probably a lot lighter than most. Not everyone gets to hear a tearful apology from their rapist, as I eventually did. Not everyone has the kind of parents that will love them at their very worst, and still somehow see the very best in them. And not everyone that loses their faith comes back to it. I am grateful to say that I did.

This is a story about forgiveness. Not forgiveness for my rapist as much as finding the ability to forgive myself. Within these words, I'll take you back in time to everything that led up to what happened, the unraveling of me, and finally, how I eventually came back to life. These words are quite literally my diary. They are raw, they are real, and they are being placed before you for one purpose…to provide a light in the dark. I think the worst part of being in a mental prison from such an event is the loneliness and inescapable self-blame.

My journey to freeing myself from the demons that were born into my head during these rough times in my life was a long one. I may sound utterly crazy or wildly stupid as you read the mess that became of me, and that's okay because I can honestly say, I was both of those things at times. My only hope in sharing my story is to say, no matter what you've done to cope with your pain, how far you've fallen from who you were, it's never too late to be who you are now, because who you are now is enough. I believe that God holds all of our tears and our pieces, and if we let Him, He will turn them into something more beautiful than we ever imagined. And if you don't believe in God, that's okay…He believes in you.

So, let's start at the beginning. About eleven years ago…

The Breakup

I remember the breakup. Finally, the never-ending relationship from high school came to an end. No more toxic psycho family to deal with, no more worrying if my boyfriend was going to be able to get himself up and to work in the morning, no more worrying about him not taking care of himself, and best of all, no more worrying about literally everything else under the sun apart from myself.

After my boyfriend left his abusive family, I thought he might have had a shot at a better life. He does seem happy now, and I'm very grateful for that because even though our relationship finally came to an end after four long years, he will always be family to me after the way he loved mine. He deserved so much more from his own, and despite their ugliness, I will never have regrets about the four years we spent together.

14 years old to almost 19…first kiss…first *almost* everything. The biggest surprise to everyone would be…I was still a virgin when we split. Everyone, including his family, assumed that was not the case, but the truth is, we never quite crossed that line. That's not to say that we didn't try, but I guess you could say I just wasn't ever able to fully relax enough for that to happen, and he was very gentle with me. Something I would later miss.

I never expected to get into Westwood Christian University, yet I didn't apply anywhere else. My GPA was good, but my ACT sucked. Writing skills were my thing, and my paper and GPA got me in the door. I was so excited when I received the news that I got in. I had been so stressed with my personal life, mainly with making sure my boyfriend, who was a year older than me, landed on his feet. I had also been helping take care of my grandparents since I was 15 and I was always knee-deep in whatever was going on with my family. My boyfriend had helped me take care of them on my weekend shifts, too. That was part of what kept me so bonded to him; his heart was pure.

To this day, I'll never forget what he said one morning on his way to work after he was living on his own. He had brought donuts by, and I was still in bed, so he talked with my parents in the living room. He said that the only reason he believed in God was because of me. That in itself was enough for me to hold no regrets with us and all we went through together. But something interesting happened when we split…something no one saw coming who knew me well. I got over it in a matter of two days.

My family fully expected that if we ever finally came to an end, I would be wrecked for months and months to come based on how attached at the hip he and I were. I had lost 15 pounds during high school when we had split once before. But something was different this time…I think I finally saw that even being away from his family wasn't going to change the fundamental differences between us and what I needed in a life partner. So, I cried for a couple of days, and was released from it somehow.

The toxicity of his family had been such a tremendous burden, and the repercussions that affected him also affected me, and frankly my family too. When I realized he needed to go further down a road that wasn't for me, I finally had enough self-respect to rise above it. I'm proud of the person he is today, and we are still friends, but there was a short chapter where that wasn't the case, and it gave me the room to breathe and the room to see everything for what it was. I realized that I had a future outside of him. That sounds obvious and even silly to say, but first loves can really feel like your whole world. Especially when you want to save them from such an abusive situation; having that in the mix amplified my feelings into a role that never should have been mine.

It's hard when you carry someone else. It's so easy to lose sight of who you are. My family had been there for him more than his own ever had in those few years, and while they cared about him very much, they worried that all of this was taking too heavy of a toll on me. I was relieved for them to see me finally blossoming after the split. I always carried so much guilt for all the unnecessary drama that came with being in that relationship.

I felt lighter than I had in years when we finally called it quits; I was able to see myself for the first time in so long…and it's going to sound weird to say, but I couldn't stop smiling. Between my family and him, I didn't make much room for many friendships in my life. I decided to change that with my new free time and rekindle with some of my friends from when he and I had split for a few months in high school. Jamie and I had technically known each other since we were 12. He met me at my most awkward stage…my innocence was beyond intact.

We had just moved here from the West Coast after I had done a homeschooling phase for two years during all of our moving and my grandmother's illness battles. Needless to say, the innocence and homeschooling showed *a lot*. And it didn't take long before I became a target for bullying. I handled it pretty well with my newly found sarcasm, but it was a very lonely time for me. Not at all what I expected when I moved to the south…I expected some charming Southern bells. Church didn't work out well for me either after they switched the staffing around; the woman who took over our youth group almost seemed to dislike kids. My only two other friendships that were out of state imploded with time and revealing circumstances.

Jamie was one of the few people that had always stood the test of time with his kindness. We had some laughs in high school, but never really talked much outside of random events. I called him and told him what happened, and he instantly got me connected with some other friends I had known in school. One of those friends was named Charlie.

The Three Musketeers

Charlie had always had these amazing bonfires at his house, and back when I had my old Bronco, I'd take the top down, grab friends and head over there to hang out. It was always a memorable night. Jamie called him and told him that my ex and I had finally split, and he called me up to check in on me. I was flattered and excited when he invited me to a bonfire he was throwing like old times for Halloween.

Jamie was supposed to bring me but had a date come up instead, so I drove myself, and we all rekindled. There were several people there, but at the end of the night, it was just me, Charlie, Jamie and his date whom I can't remember…Jennifer or Jessie. Anyway, the girl started snoring louder than you can imagine when the three of us were still awake and trying to go to sleep in Charlie's basement. Jamie randomly said, "Oh my God…" and we couldn't stop laughing. That was the beginning of what I call "The Three Musketeer phase" of our friendship.

Me, Charlie, and Jamie became inseparable for the next few months. And I was the happiest I had been in years. The memories that unfolded were so special to me. It was like I finally got to be a kid, and the best part was, it was innocent fun. We didn't drink, we didn't do drugs…the humor may have been a little off-color at times, and we pretty much always stayed out until 2 in the morning, but it was always the best time. It was everything I had missed out on in high school and then some.

I had known that Charlie's stepmother went to high school with my ex's mother, so I did warn him that he may end up hearing negative things about me, but nothing seemed to come of that for the first few months. And even if it had, I sensed that Charlie was a true friend who would set the record straight on my behalf.

Jamie and Charlie were very different personalities, but I felt like we all molded together somehow, and I was so grateful to have them by my side. Jamie was the listener; I could vent to him for hours, and he'd put up with every bit of it. He was also the one who would say the most hilarious things when you'd least expect it; his stories (true or not) always had me cracking up. He would zip around town with his ginormous subs in his Suburu WRX and be the goober I always needed to be able to unwind from school and any reminisce of past relational drama with my ex's family.

We'd come to a red light and blare songs like Take on Me or Jump Around, and it would make my day to see a stranger's reaction to us expressing our weirdness so shamelessly. To this day, I'm pretty confident that we would gladly get our crazy on at a red light to the same songs right on cue.

And then there was Charlie, in his Chevy, always ready to go off-roading at any time of the day or night. He would say the most outlandish things that would have me laughing when I needed it, too. He also had a love for music and would play guitar and sing, which I thought was cool. He was not the person I would talk to about deep things or anything really outside of in-the-moment stuff, but he had a way about him that kept me on my toes. And my instincts told me he was an awkward but pure soul…kind of like me. He would just show up at my house unannounced and act like he was family, joining in on whatever we were doing. And I loved it.

I loved finally being able to enjoy friendships and laugh so hard that it brought tears to my eyes almost every time we hung out. I loved our adventures. I loved that I no longer felt like a prisoner of so many things that were out of my control. Jamie and Charlie became my daily bliss in some way or another. Inappropriate jokes and all. And I felt a peace in my heart with no strings attached for the first time since we had moved here.

After the Halloween party at Charlie's with the snorer, we kept at our usual bonfires, going to the movies, and spending time at Charlie's house or my parent's house. My 19th birthday was just around the corner, and it was probably to date, one of the best birthdays I've ever had at the hands of friends. Charlie had brought Pete, who was going through a rough time (I'll get into more about him later), and Jamie had picked me up, and we all met at Charlie's. They bought steaks, canned stuff and things to make a fire, and we all hopped in Charlie's truck and drove out into the woods through the neighborhood behind his house. The boys built a fire and cooked these steaks with sticks and literally ate them…a few bites, anyway. Their faces were too priceless not to capture with that first bite.

Pete was only with us at the beginning of the night, and then Charlie took him back to his parents and joined us again. I remember them singing 'Happy Birthday' to me and us laughing a lot that night. Even though I took a hard pass on the steaks, I was so touched that they did that for me. We said a birthday cheers with our glass Colas and went four-wheeling after our fire died down. I was in heaven.

New Boyfriend

A semi-close girlfriend of mine, Jessica, had known that I was single and decided to try and hook me up with one of her friends (Ralph) for a double date. She and her boyfriend had been dating for a minute, and Ralph and Jessica had known each other for at least a year or so before this. We hit it off, and I was so surprised that I was able to feel anything for anyone after just coming out of such a long relationship. But I did. We decided to make it official even with the long-distance dating situation.

He went to school over three hours away, and he was only in town for his Thanksgiving break when we got together originally. Over the coming weeks, we texted and called daily, and when he was home, we went to each other's houses. And I, of course, introduced him to Jamie and Charlie, whom Jessica also knew from high school.

Lots of fun memories ensued, and I got to the point where I was genuinely so happy that I couldn't stop singing every time I was alone. I couldn't believe my life had gone from this dark and dim place for so long to this wide-open space filled with nothing but hope and excitement. I was even managing to make a 4.0 GPA at Westwood…something I never dreamed I'd accomplish. My blank canvas brought me unexplainable joy. I remember pinching myself, thinking, *you can't be this happy*…something has to give at some point. I just wish I hadn't been right.

I remember that I began to get calls from Charlie nearly every day during my first class, and he even showed up on campus one day at random. He managed to find my truck, park by it and wait for the shuttle to come crash a class with me. It made my day that he wanted to spend time with me enough to go through the effort to make it happen…I wasn't used to that. I also had some mild drama beginning with Ralph as he was ready to move faster than I wanted in our new relationship.

I didn't feel as strongly for him, mainly because the timing was so short, and I had such a balance in my life…I wasn't ready to give my whole heart when I was just finding myself again. I wanted to stay in my happy bubble and soak it all up. And I was honest about that when he wanted me to transfer schools within the first few weeks of dating…too much too fast began to creep up on me, and I began to push him away. But, if I'm honest, that wasn't the only reason I pushed him away.

Complicated

In addition to Ralph being too much too fast and being so easily offended that I wasn't ready for that much so quickly, I had begun falling for my best friend. And some small part of me thought he was falling for me, too. I had gotten to know Charlie more and more as we spent nearly every day together. Jamie was still with us a lot of the time, too, but Charlie would just show up, and it began to be a comfort to me, knowing he would just be there.

I'll never forget my chapel credits. I had a few I needed to make up, but they were only available to make up at night. Charlie would have me pick him up from work, and we'd go together so I wouldn't have to walk in the dark to my car; he'd insist. And it would be hilarious because he'd be dressed to the nines in a suit from his place of work (Jos. A. Bank), and I'd be in sweats and a hoodie. I was always able to be myself with him.

As if that wasn't enough to start turning my head, there was this one night when he asked me to come by his work to get his credit card and go buy two toys for the Angel Tree because he had just learned it was the last night for donations. He wanted me to get one toy for a boy and one for a girl, and he didn't want to worry about the expense cap. It began to make my heart melt that he seemed so selfless and pure.

Jamie had admitted he had feelings for me on a couple of

occasions prior to Ralph and I becoming a couple, and I was starting to feel like my happy bubble was about to implode with too much emotional turmoil on the rise. I had told Jamie that our friendship was too important to me to risk losing it in a relationship, and he seemed to agree whenever that topic arose the first time. I just didn't know if he'd be as accepting of my reasoning if he knew that I was falling for Charlie. So, in order to not jeopardize my newfound happiness, I decided to ignore my feelings for Charlie to spare our friendships, and, of course, to preserve my new commitment to Ralph.

While I did genuinely feel the same way about wanting to preserve my friendship with Charlie, hiding my feelings wasn't easy…the more time we spent together, the more my heart ached to know if he felt the same way. And I began to feel more and more guilty about being in a relationship. *I know, total mess.* But the first two weeks we were dating, I would happily leave Charlie to go to Ralph's side of town when he was home, or I'd invite him to come do whatever we were doing. Heck, I remember dropping Charlie off at his truck to go meet Ralph one night because he invited me to 'pizza night' with his family. I don't know…something just changed the more I got to know him and the more I got to know Charlie. And it bothered me. I felt like I made a mistake agreeing to be Ralph's girlfriend so quickly.

Charlie's birthday rolled around, and Mom helped me throw

him a party at our house. We got him a cake, pizza, balloons, and a ton of silly string that we attacked him with. We had a blast, and I could tell it meant a lot to him in his way. After we finished having cake, he wanted to go to this beautiful hotel that had a gorgeous Christmas light display. It was a popular place to go in our city, and this was the first time I had ever been. It was me, Jamie, and Charlie's friend Daniel. He drove us in my car…he always drove even if we were in my SUV. We blared music that I can still hear to this day in my mind when I think back on how special that night felt.

After the hotel lights, we went to this giant arcade and took silly pictures, and then he wanted to drive us out to Infinite Circle, where he said his dad proposed to his stepmom. It was a pretty hilltop where you could see a full skyline view of our city. The music we listened to on the way home was slower, deeper, and I felt so full of joy to be right in the moment where I was…utterly happy. Even with how stupid and silly we were 90 percent of the time, there was always this 10 percent where things felt as real as the lyrics we listened to. Nights like that led my heart to believe that we'd have each other's backs forever.

The next morning, Charlie was his usual obnoxious self and had shown up at my parent's house unannounced when I was still in my PJs. He got himself a bowl of cereal and literally invited himself to join mom and me at the movies. He seemed to make her laugh, too.

After we got home, she needed us to run to the store to get stuff for dinner (which we assumed he would be staying for at this point). We hopped in his truck and went off to the store, but on the way there, in front of my parents' neighborhood, there was a new development in process across the street. He floored it over there, and we went mudding. There wasn't one inch of his truck that wasn't caked with mud. And then, the unfortunate but hilarious thing happened…we got ourselves stuck. And I mean, really stuck! He had to get a board of wood he had in the bed of the truck and try to wedge it under one of his tires. He had to take his shirt off and literally lay under the truck in the mud to accomplish this.

I couldn't stop laughing at him while simultaneously apologizing for not being able to get under there and help; I was wearing one of Ralph's shirts he had lent me while he was away at school, and I didn't want to ruin it. I'll never forget him sarcastically laughing and cussing about it, "Ralph's shirt, Ralph's f**king shirt, are you f**king kidding me?!" Then he started randomly singing "every little thing's gonna be alright" while he finished getting the board wedged under his tire. I had Three Little Birds stuck in my head for days after watching the video I took of our muddy trip to the store. He tied the front of the truck up with some rope to a nearby tree in front of us, and we were finally able to get some traction and get out of there. We still went to the store too, covered in mud. I'm sure they appreciated that…

I was falling for him. And I could not help it at that point. *Wrong, I know*. But I kept thinking on all of it and I guess for me, I looked at Charlie and saw this big-hearted Christian guy that wanted to make me laugh and change the world for the better. And when I looked at Ralph, I knew he wasn't a Christian, we had nothing politically in common, and he had really turned me off with how demanding he was of my future when we had only been dating a few very short weeks. It was becoming too much. We didn't know each other long enough for him to have irritable episodes with me and those were becoming more frequent every time we spoke. Charlie literally called me and came to see me almost daily and brought the opposite to the table; he was lighthearted, easy to talk to, and while he could be obnoxious, he was never demanding. My heart just didn't stand a chance after Ralph began picking at me.

I'm not sure if Jamie was attending school out of town at this point or not, but I don't remember him being around as much outside of weekends. When he was home, the three of us continued to always spend time together. With Charlie, we'd get pizza, watch movies at my parents, hang at his, and even went to church together once; he also invited me over for this big lunch with his family. There were so many of them visiting from out of town. I remember it being super awkward because everyone kept asking me/us if we were dating, and I kept having to say I was dating someone else.

One afternoon, I had been sitting at home and got this abrupt call from Charlie. He was going to see his mom in Arizona for a few days, and he had left his guitar in his truck. He was hoping that, by some miracle, we could bring his guitar to the airport before his flight. I called Jamie since he had the sportier car, and we both booked it over to Charlie's. I found his hidden key and straddled his guitar on my lap while Jamie drove as fast as we could. We got there 20 minutes or less before his flight.

Charlie came running out in his socks to retrieve it, and it became quite a memorable moment. We laughed about that for days. I remember his mom messaging me to thank us for making that happen so they could hear him sing and play for them during his visit.

Charlie always loved to wrestle and goof off, and both he and Jamie used to spank me and things along that line in joking. I never really thought much of it. I grew up with like 12 boys in my old neighborhood, and I always loved to play rough. I had also trained in MMA throughout my childhood, so I was hardly what you'd call 'fragile'. But the bruises from all the times Charlie and I goofed off like that were beginning to show a lot more. I remember I had this bruise on my arm that was so big, people kept asking me about it at work.

I had taken a job at Hollister over Christmas break because Jamie and Charlie both worked at the mall, and I thought it would be fun to make some extra cash and still get to see them on breaks and stuff. I remember Charlie coming in to see me one day when I was reorganizing a bunch of clothes on the floor, and everyone kept pegging me in front of him, asking if he was my boyfriend. I denied it, of course, but I wanted to study his face at the sound of that to see what his reaction would be.

He had always verbalized his type, and I clearly wasn't it. I used to wonder if he intentionally wanted me to know that I was not his type. And I'll be honest-looks wise, he was not my type *at all* either. In fact, I never had a crush on him in the prior years we had known each other. Frankly, it wasn't until the Angel Tree, my chapel credits, and him just showing up nearly every day that he caught my eye in that way. Even the guitar and singing bit didn't serenade my heart at all. It was the thought of his heart and mine being the same. Sadly, I was way off base. I wish I had been more discerning of his other behaviors instead of just writing him off as a bit awkward, like myself.

The first time looking back that I remember him being weird was when we were alone in his basement wrestling (which I know was weird in itself at our age, but I was crushing, and I enjoyed goofing off with him like that so we could be closer). He started to get a bad headache out of the blue, and he laid his head on my lap and said something about us having kids… a very odd thing for him to bring up at random.

It never came up again, and I didn't bring it up either. It really seemed like he didn't mean to say whatever his exact words were out loud, and because I was with Ralph, I knew it would be inappropriate to fish to find out what brought that to his mind. But the weirdest thing was what happened after he said that…he started randomly biting me, like hard! I didn't know what to make of that. Still don't. I just remember awkwardly calling him out for being so strange and asking him to stop.

The more I've reflected on this chapter of my life, the more memories have surfaced that were peppered in with odd occurrences like that with Charlie. Yet, I don't remember my feelings wavering much at that point in time. I just felt like I was in a triangle of mixed emotions, and while I cherished my uncomplicated happiness, I knew I couldn't cover up where my heart was leading me for much longer. There was no denying that my feelings for Ralph were dissipating while my feelings for Charlie were increasing. I didn't know what to do. And in the back of my mind, I was still worried knowing that Jamie had said stuff about his affection for me because I wanted to preserve our "three musketeers" relationship.

Jamie is still a friend in my life to this day. Truth is, the main reason I was never attracted to him was most likely because of the girls he'd tell me he'd been with in detail. It grossed me out. I just kept picturing STDs and couldn't get past the 'player' aspect that came with him.

Oddly enough, Charlie was exerting some of the same behaviors and, in fact, took it to another level by having me go with him to get Plan B for a one-night stand he had. That should have been a big turn-off that lasted in my mind, but he seemed like he was utterly disappointed in himself, and I didn't get the impression he slept around regularly. I was not dating Ralph at the time that occurred, nor did I have feelings for Charlie yet. In the weeks that followed that night, Charlie kept talking about his interest in mission trips and wanting to make a difference in the world. I knew he was an up-and-coming Christian and hadn't grown up in a Christian home, so I always wanted to be encouraging and meet him where he was at.

In the few weeks between October and December, I felt like I saw nothing but goodness in Charlie. His humor was raunchy at times, and the rough play sometimes left me with some unwanted markings, but I always remember laughing and feeling like I was the best version of myself when we were together.

The drives to and from school on my favorite backroad filled my spirit with a purifying element that freed me from my past sadness. Freedom from the sadness over my ex-boyfriend and his abusive family, freedom from the sadness of watching my grandmother and, by in stretch, my whole family suffer with her illness for 6 long years, and most of all, freedom from the loneliness that used to hold me so tightly. All of these things that once succumbed my heart no longer had a hold on me, and I blamed this beautiful friendship I had stumbled into.

My only dilemma was figuring out what to do with all of these emotions amidst my actual relationship with Ralph and my friendship with Jamie. And, of course, the truth was, I had absolutely no idea if Charlie even had feelings for me in that way. What I did know was, I didn't want to lose *this*. This revived version of myself that I had never been able to be.

On Christmas Eve, I invited the guys over for some sauce and to watch Tommy Boy. Ralph and I had been having tension over the lack of attention I was giving our relationship and how irritable he had become with me. I just wasn't ready for anything serious yet, especially not with the unknowns happening in my heart. So, when he began pushing harder for more of my time, I backpedaled, and the rest is history.

Jamie and Charlie both stopped by for a few hours, and we enjoyed some time together and that got my mind off the drama I had been trying to avoid. I had hoped we'd make that a tradition going forward. I was so grateful that my parents were so welcoming and accommodating; growing up, all of my friends used to tell me that they wished my parents could adopt them. They have always had the biggest hearts, and their love for others has always carried a depth that most lack. At this point in my life, my parents were so relieved to see me finally smiling, stress-free, and genuinely happy for the first time in years. And I was so elated to be able to give them that peace. They deserved that and so much more.

On Christmas day, Ralph and I officially decided to call it quits. And as much as I felt bad as I heard the frustration in his voice, I remember feeling relieved because I knew he deserved someone I couldn't be for him. He was a sweet guy, and I held no regrets with the few weeks we dated because he made me laugh and was a total gentleman (something Charlie definitely was not, actually). He gave me a short, but normal experience with no dreadful strings attached. I had hoped we'd stay friends, which I'm thankful to say we did and are to this day.

Heartbeat

On December 27th, my parents had been planning to leave town with friends to go to the Biltmore for a two-night stay. My grandmother had passed away about two years before this, and my grandfather was now living with us because his Parkinsons had gotten worse when he was living in a retirement home. He decided he'd rather be with us, and we were happy he wanted to. We tried to preserve his independence, seeing as the basement had a kitchenette and a lot of private space for him to do many things within his comfort zone. I was going to be home for the two days my parents were out of town to ensure if he fell, I could help him. I planned to keep him company and bring him meals and such.

My grandfather was my best pal growing up, and we had always been close. I loved him so much, and my whole life leading up to this time frame, I had been so close to my family; I never aspired to change that. I didn't desire to move away or to have my own life separate from them. I wanted them to be a part of all of it.

My grandfather chose to retire to spend more time with me when I was little, and part of why I wanted to stay close to home was to give the same back to him. My mom was always my ultimate best friend and the voice I counted on most. And my dad was always there for me, even with a hectic work schedule. I loved our small but strong family. We had taken on so many setbacks together and always found ways to laugh through it all. I felt like Charlie and Jamie were such special gifts in my life because they loved how close I was to my family, and they were never afraid to join in.

My parents had never left town before, and I felt like if there was ever a time to stray away from my road of innocence in a way I was comfortable, this was it. Mind you, I had never had a drop of alcohol. I had never partied. I had never done much of anything in that department at all. So, when I got wind of them leaving, I decided to invite Charlie and Jamie to stay the night with me. When that was propositioned, Charlie decided to see if his uncle would get us some alcohol. His uncle ended up getting us a bottle of cheap silver tequila.

It was a casual night, amongst other things. After I brought my grandfather his dinner, I came back upstairs to test out the tequila; I put a movie on in the background. We had this special edition Mountain Due for a chaser, and I remember not needing to chase down my shots, or at least pretending like I didn't. I had about 3 shots worth and didn't really feel that drunk. I remember acting like I was when I chose to eat popcorn off the Christmas tree to make the guys laugh. They tried to "take care of me" by heating me up some food, but somehow ended up putting silverware in the microwave and breaking it. Eventually, they began to drink more, and then they got really quiet. No one seemed to be that into the movie, and it was getting late, so I asked them if they wanted to go to bed.

As I'm typing this, tears fill my eyes because I'm just so sorry for my Grandpa and how I wasn't there for him the way I should have been that night. I know he didn't technically "need" anything, but I just wish I had stayed true to myself and gone downstairs and watched a movie with him instead of this whole stupid plan I came up with. And my dog? Where was my sweet boy? I'm sure I cuddled him and made sure he had food and water, but it makes me sick to my stomach to think about how distracted I was that night with my selfish desires.

Charlie had ridden with Jamie and we parked his car in the garage in case my neighbors were to see because I didn't want my parents to assume the worst or be embarrassed by me. I think some part of me felt entitled to do this because I had never done anything like this before. I also felt safe with my guys; they were my friends, after all, right? I cherished the fact that I felt safe with them. Having friends like this was something my lonely heart had always hoped I'd eventually find.

I finally turned the movie off, and we headed to my room. Once in bed, Jamie was on my right, Charlie was on my left, and I eventually laid my head towards Charlie's side, but I was still on my own pillow in the middle. A few minutes seemed to pass like this, and it was so quiet. I was pining away in my heart, hoping that Chalie would give me some sign he felt something for me. He knew I was single again. He knew we had both been drinking a bit…if there was ever a time, I figured this was it. And I was right…he reached his left hand over to my chin and tilted my lips up to meet his, and he kissed me. He kissed me for a long minute before placing my hand on his heart. I wasn't sure what he was doing at first, but when his eyes met mine, I felt how fast his heart was beating…I could tell that was his way of showing me he was nervous.

He was one hundred percent vulnerable in this moment with me. I began to feel overcome with all these feelings I had been pushing back in the weeks leading up to this night. I was so caught up in everything that I dismissed Jamie's feelings. Charlie got up out of bed and held onto my hand and guided me out to the living room with him. He picked me up and laid me on the couch, got on top of me, and began making out with me. We both seemed equally passionate for one another, and my heart was so taken in all of it.

A couple of minutes later, out walked Jamie from my room and saw us making out on the couch; we both felt terrible (at least I think Charlie did too) as we stopped abruptly. Jamie was practically in tears, and I felt like the worst friend in the world. The two of them ended up sitting in his car, talking in the garage for 20 minutes. After they returned inside, the three of us sat and talked in the living room for a long time. Oddly enough, we didn't really talk much about our kissing that I can remember off-hand. It sounds familiar to say we played it off a bit and acted like we were just friends who were drinking and got caught up in the moment or something along those lines. I remember trying to let Charlie lead that because I was curious what he would say. Jamie asked if we had been seeing each other like that, and we explained that this was the first time.

Not long after that was said, Charlie began to share some stuff he had done in the past that he thought made him a horrible person and some awful stuff that he believed happened to him, too. I don't really remember what Jamie said about us because everything Charlie began to say changed the tone of the conversation dramatically. The minimal remaining awkwardness seemed to leave the room as we zeroed in on Charlie's words. I remember him talking about his childhood. I knew that his dad cheated on his mom with his current stepmom and that they married and had two children, a boy and a girl.

The girl was the youngest by a few years, and I may have parts of what he shared wrong, but it sounded like he touched his half-sister inappropriately when he was 12. She was somewhere around age 7 or 8 at the time. He said this like it were some dark and depraved act that he plotted out, and I recall trying to comfort him with the reality that all kids are born curious about stuff and explore.

I had two experiences where I was touched inappropriately by other kids myself at age 6 and age 8, but I don't think that the kids that did it were trying to molest or hurt me; they were going through periods of curiosity. They were 3-4 years older than me too. After trying to bring him some comfort from my personal experiences, he got a little deeper as to why he thought he did it. He said that his grandfather (I'm unsure which side of the family) had touched him inappropriately when he was little (around age 9).

Needless to say, the depth of that confession brought us to a whole new level. We began trying to comfort him about that and told him how sick and evil that was. I also remember trying to make sure that he understood the difference between what he did and what his grandfather did, and frankly, how he may have been partially curious because of what happened to him.

I don't remember anything else discussed that night, but we went back to my bedroom eventually and went to sleep. I didn't know what to think about what had just happened between Charlie and me after what became of the night, and I didn't know if Jamie's reaction changed how Charlie felt. I wondered if he really had feelings and if he did, could they lead anywhere for us? I remember asking them to be super quiet when they left the next morning and begged Jamie not to rev his engine or play anything loud in hopes that my neighbors wouldn't see. Shortly after seeing them off, my head was spinning with what had happened the night before. Things seemed back to normal, but I didn't know what that meant; would they stay that way, or would Charlie and I talk about what happened between us at some point?

Lust

I went about my morning, threw on some sweats, and made my grandfather breakfast and talked with him for a bit. A couple of hours (if that) passed, and suddenly Charlie called me. He acted one hundred percent casual and normal with me…super upbeat, finishing my sentences, loud, sarcastic, everything per the usual. At first, I was a little taken back by that and even a bit sad, but then I realized I was simultaneously grateful that we were good even if the topic of 'us' didn't come up. I knew if nothing more were to come from what had just happened between us, I'd be okay as long as we still had our friendship.

He informed me that he was almost at my house, taking an early lunch break and asked if I had any more food. He came in and helped himself to some cereal, and we talked in the living room about random things for a few minutes. When he was done eating, he put his bowl on the coffee table. Suddenly, he came over to me, picked me up and put me right back on the couch where we had been making out the night before. We were kissing very intimately like we picked up right where we left off, but this time things were a little different. I felt him rub his hand against my pants in a rough and abrupt way, and it took me off guard that he was already leaping into that so quickly. It caused me to pause and sit up. I told him I needed to ask him something, and I could tell that made him uncomfortable. He wasn't sure where I was taking this. And that reaction already made me feel unsure of things between us.

I asked him what this meant to him. His response was fairly quick, and if I'm honest, it cut like a knife. He said it was just more of a "lust" thing. *Ouch.* I told him something along the lines of "Yeah, well, I'm sorry, but I can't do this then. I'm a relationship kind of girl." And within 3 minutes of me saying that, he was gone. Before he left, he said something about "needing time to view me like I was back in the friend zone again." I remember being so unbelievably hurt that he didn't have real feelings for me and that, frankly, he would have just treated me like some random hook up in spite of what *I thought* was a genuine friendship. I was glad to know that before things went further at the same time.

Things only got worse from there. He became extremely weird about the whole situation. He began avoiding me completely, and it made me wish we had never kissed to begin with. I missed him. And I began to hate how much I missed him. He asked me to "keep the group" (our small circle of bonfire friends) together while he was "away" and told me he would "meditate" and try to get his mind back in the friend zone when it came to me. *Very odd.* But again, I was still trying to swallow this big bundle of feelings I had developed for him, and I didn't put as much effort into processing his strange behavior as I should have. There was this ginormous gap in the next few days that followed where he had always been, and it was making me feel so empty.

New Year's Eve was approaching, and I invited the group, including him, over to the house to celebrate. I told him to get over whatever this was and come have fun with us. Of course, deep down, I kept secretly hoping he'd take back his lust comment and want to be more. I tried on like 3 outfits and, for once, put a lot of effort into my makeup. He came, and I don't remember much about the night, but nothing happened between us. I remember having a pit in my stomach because he seemed so intentionally distant from me. This was now the beginning of 2013, and oh, how I wish I had known this was only the beginning of my pain when it came to this guy.

January 10th, 2013

The next several days made me feel even worse. It was like our new normal was barely speaking via text or some random two-minute empty call. I tried to just focus on school and accept that whatever happened between us meant two different things to him versus me. While I had prepared to accept the idea of us never being a couple for a multitude of reasons, past and now present, I never thought I'd have to prepare myself to lose our friendship. That's exactly how it felt…like he was taking his friendship away from me. And it hurt me that it seemed so easy for him. I felt like an idiot and like I had completely misjudged everything. Especially him.

Well, randomly, on January 10th, I go into my first class (English), and I see our picture from my birthday pop up on my phone. My heart leapt. He hadn't really been calling me much since all of this happened between us. I didn't know what to expect when I called him back. For all I knew, he needed a favor like the other night. I remembered feeling the same relief three days prior to this when he called me around 8 o'clock at night. But, to my dismay, it wasn't to hang out or talk or anything; it was because he needed fifty bucks to pay a locksmith to break into his truck for him. He locked his keys in his truck randomly a lot. I was a little disappointed that it was over money, of course, but I jumped at the chance to go see him, hoping things would start to go back to normal.

He had been playing guitar on the main street in our small-town segment of the city, about a 30-minute drive away from me. When I got there, he was still acting odd, and I don't think he even really thanked me for the money. I remember leaving not long after I got there because I couldn't take how much this continued weirdness between us was hurting me.

So, with the unknowns of how this was going to go, I was reluctant to call him back after my class on the 10th, but I did. And to my pleasant surprise, he seemed more like his old self. He wasn't calling me because he needed anything, he was calling because he wanted to meet me at my house to hang out. I remember he said he was planning to be there by noon, so I decided to skip my last two classes that day because I was so relieved that he was being normal again. I just wanted my friend back.

I pulled up around noon, and he was waiting on the bed of his truck in my driveway. I remember feeling a little insecure at this point because I was afraid that he would get weird again, so I was more guarded at first. But, sure enough, things really felt normal after the first hour or two passed, and I was more caught up in that relief than anything else.

He had been talking about wanting to go on a mission trip to Africa, and I remember that being something we talked about doing together at one point. Obviously, if we were ever to have gone on such a trip, we wouldn't have needed survival training, but nonetheless, he was a guy. Guys love trying to pretend they are on the set of 'Survivor.' He used the idea of going on a trip there as an excuse to practice survival tactics, which meant buying a new saw to get more savvy with cutting wood for bonfires. After we bought one at Lowes, we drove to the big mall in town and looked around at Bass Pro for survival gear and fun stuff for camping. A few hours later, we ended up back at my house, and my mom made dinner while he used our computer to sign up for his classes at State. I guess State started later than Westwood did.

The details of the night are a bit of a blur from here. I vaguely remember saying a prayer over dinner and making small talk with him and Mom and Dad. I remember us talking about going out into the woods and wanting to bring lights and some towels because we were going to have a small bonfire and likely make smores or something like that. I don't really remember the drive out there, but I know that it was tucked way back where we used to always go four-wheeling in a neighborhood that wasn't fully developed yet. You could get to this place from the back of Charlie's property through the neighborhood behind it (which was older) or by going through the newer side of this development a little further down in front of the semi-new elementary school.

It was probably around 9 or 10 when we went out there. I didn't have classes the next morning, but I figured he had work, so we probably couldn't stay too long. I was wearing a T-shirt and jeans, and Mom had lent me her brown hiking boots for the mud. It wasn't as cold as it had been, but it was still hoodie weather, so we had sweatshirts. We got there and started to build a fire like any other night; the only difference was we hadn't ever done this alone before. Normally, if we built a fire, it was for our group or at least Jamie and us. But I was so happy we were here doing this. I thought maybe if we were alone long enough, he'd talk to me about what was up with his mental state the last two weeks. Nothing really came up, though, and I was afraid to ruin the night with some awkward moment in search of answers.

The fire felt amazing because as it got closer to 11, the temperature continued to drop. Suddenly, we heard coyotes off in the distance, but they began to sound a little too close for comfort. Charlie abruptly acted like we should run and get in the truck, and I remember us laughing about it as the howls seemed to be creeping up on us. We sat in there for a couple of minutes (if it was even that long). I don't remember anything being said leading up to this moment; I just remember him leaning over to my side and making out with me passionately. And I don't know why I didn't stop him this time or say anything about his prior "lust" commentary. I guess I just figured he must have been shy before or was afraid to tell me he had feelings for me.

His touch instantly captivated me because my feelings had

never really changed, even though I was confused by his actions in the weeks leading up to this. Clothes began to come off. He came over to my side and got on the bottom, and I was laying on his chest topless as we started making out again. We laughed a couple of times, and I even said it was weird making out with my best friend and being half-naked laying on him, but I meant it in a cute way…thinking we were simply growing our friendship into a relationship.

I could feel myself getting carried away, and when he eventually tried getting my pants down and wanted me to get in the back, I began to clench up a bit. I had only been with one guy all through high school, and we rarely got to the point that Charlie and I were at within a matter of minutes. It also never developed into full on sex in my past relationship. Charlie didn't know I was still a virgin, and in fact, he used to always make stupid jokes and would ask the size of my ex's penis when we first broke up. He and Jamie both had really immature moments like that. But again, my bad judgment just ruled that off as guys being guys, and I didn't hold his character accountable like I should have done many times looking back now.

I was starting to get really nervous as he climbed into the backseat and pulled me back with him. I was now down to my underwear because when I scooched into the back, he helped take my pants all the way down and off of me. I didn't object to that, but

I knew that I was letting this go too far, and I wanted to make sure he understood that we couldn't go all the way. I began to say that to him when he climbed on top of me. And, of course, I expected that my words meant something to him; after all, he cared about me, right? He was my friend…

I remember saying "no" many times when he kept reaching to pull my underwear off. I had to physically move his hand several times when he kept ignoring me. The more that I kept having to say no and push his hand away, the more uncomfortable I started to become. Making out and testing the limits with him began to lose its pleasure. I was beginning to worry that he didn't understand me when I kept saying "no," so I wanted to make it extra clear by verbalizing that I didn't want to have sex. I remember trying to get him to look at me and see my face when I said, "Charlie, this is going to have to be enough for you, okay?" His reply was, "You know you want to."

I remember being afraid to ruin anything between us and I said something back along the lines of yes, I would, but we can't. The truth is, I probably would have very quickly worked up to wanting to have sex with him had he asked me to be his and treated me like I was worth something to him. Even though I knew that went against what I believed in and what I promised my family, I would have likely gone the distance with him and asked for forgiveness later because I was so taken with this guy for reasons I don't even understand. Sadly, Charlie didn't really care about me. I just didn't know it yet.

The way he persisted and pushed me to change my mind even after I said *no* so many times began to make me question all of it…maybe I was wrong to think he had a change of heart about the "lust" category he had put me in. Losing our friendship again, how cold and iced out he made me feel in the days prior to this, my racing heart, my vulnerability…all of these things were crossing my mind in this small span of time as I lay there, unsure how to put a stop to this without making things weird with us again.

Before I could say anything else, he very quickly took my underwear off or slid them to the side (it's a blur) and rammed me, for lack of a better word. I just remember my head bumping into the rear driver's side door with each thrust as I lay there in shock that he was doing this to me after every single effort I made to tell him I didn't want this. I came to it for a second from the shock, and I was shaking as I said his name and pushed his chest up off of me; I made sure he and I locked eyes when I said, "Charlie, I can't do this." And I'll never forget his response. He looked down and smiled at me, and said, "We already are." He reentered me abruptly and finished within less than a minute as I just laid there, eyes wide, head still hitting the door as pieces within depths of me were shattered. I had just made one of the biggest mistakes of my life in thinking I could trust my friend. And thinking I ever really mattered to him.

And to make matters worse, the words he said after this couldn't have been more cruel and cutting. He said things like, "Don't look at me naked" (completely cold and causal) as he leapt back into the front seat. And "Man, I'd never want to do that again." I felt like used trash. A box checked off. Meaningless. As I was trying to take in all of the ugliness flying at me from a million different directions, I don't remember saying much of anything. I had basically shut down as I just sat back there, naked, taking in his disgusting words. I remember that he pulled out, but thoughts of pregnancy entered my mind since there was no protection, and all it takes is one, they say. I also worried about something worse, like an STD.

After he got out of the truck, I began to pull my underwear back on and searched for the rest of my clothes. He was standing out by the fire again, and I joined him after I finally got dressed. He started talking about random things, and after a few minutes, when I didn't respond, he asked if I was okay. He noted I was being quiet. I said I was fine. I could tell my lack of speech left him worried. He knew what had just happened was wrong.

We left shortly after he made sure the fire was safe. He took me home, and the same empty, one-sided conversations filled the truck until we pulled into my driveway. It was almost like a nervous, upbeat energy took over within him; he wouldn't shut up. I don't remember saying much at all in return. He always called me dude, and now that word stung like a switchblade as he said it to me. Then to top it off, as I was leaving the truck, he said, "See you later, butt face." I didn't turn around. The heaviness in my chest burned and throbbed.

After coming in through the front door, I turned the alarm off. It was after midnight at this point, and I made my way to my room with my muddy clothes. I took Mom's boots off and started the shower. I remember scrubbing myself down there, hoping and praying I didn't have some sort of disease brewing or a pregnancy in the works. I stared at myself in the mirror, but I didn't want to look too long. I can't remember if I cried or not, and if I did, that was the one and only time that I did for a very, very long time to come.

The next day, the pit in my stomach remained until he texted me. He wanted me to meet him. Some part of me strangely found relief that he wasn't cutting me out like he did before, and yet I cringed at seeing his name. He said he wanted to talk. In case you haven't figured this out by now, I was not one of those that was immediately ready to call what happened 'rape'. In fact, it ended up taking me nearly six months to even say the word rape out loud.

I knew what he did was wrong, but I felt a lot of personal blame for allowing it to go as far as it did before speaking up. And most of all, as someone who had grown up in tap-out sparing in

MMA, I felt tremendous guilt that I didn't force him off of me. Yeah, sure, he was bigger, but I knew I could have kicked his a** if I hadn't frozen in my false trust. It wasn't like I was drunk or like he had drugged me; there was no weapon or threats involved. I couldn't compartmentalize what happened, and frankly, I remember being super upbeat, almost like I was determined not to accept it.

Plan B

As I've shared previously, my mom and I have always been super close, so she could tell something was off with me, but I covered it up. She guessed that something had happened between us; I think she thought we had sex, and I just laughed that notion off. Ironically, my mom had a gynecologist appointment that day, and I remember tagging along because we were going to go do another errand afterward. As I sat in the waiting room waiting for her, I saw all the pamphlets pertaining to every worry that was going on in my head in front of me. I wanted to approach the counter to get an appointment. I wanted someone to tell me I was fine.

I confirmed with Charlie that I would meet up with him. I can't remember where I parked my car, but I remember us meeting close by the woods because he drove us back out to the same spot. *You stupid girl.* I know…believe me, *I know*. But as weird as it sounds, I knew I wouldn't let that happen again. I thought he would apologize, and because the wounds were so fresh, I was desperate for something to bring me some comfort, even if it came from him. Truthfully…*especially* if it came from him.

Sadly, the meeting wasn't what I thought it was going to be about. It was about Plan B. The new pill they had come out with that you take after having sex without protection. The same one I had gone with him to buy for another girl a couple of months earlier.

*What. A. Dumb. A***. I felt like a total idiot for thinking this meet up was for some sort of apology. I was so warped on this whole mess that I even agreed to split it with him as if the sex that occurred was something I participated in. I remember climbing up on a tree limb from a fallen tree and walking back and forth as we discussed this.

I felt like my only option to protect what was left of my dignity was to act as though his actions didn't absolutely rip me in half. So, I played like I was fine. I had plans to go to my friend Jessica's boyfriend's house after to hang with the two of them. I technically had this as my backup plan because I wasn't sure what was going to happen with our talk. I was grateful to have plans because not only was there no apology or remorse from him in our conversation, but to top it off, he treated the whole situation as if it were just another day.

We drove separately to the pharmacy and parked by each other. Another fun bonus was that he couldn't go in to buy it with me because he had his two labs with him in the bed of the truck. To this day, I can't stand having to drive by that CVS. Oh, and I had to wear my knee-high leather-heeled boots because my sneakers got trashed from going back out into the woods, and those were the only spare shoes I had in my car for whatever reason. I was mortified when I handed the pharmacist my I.D.; I looked like I had just called it a night from my shift on 3rd avenue.

We sat in the parking lot, and I opened it up. I was intimidated by this pill because I didn't know what to expect. As I put it in my mouth and grabbed my water, I said, "Cheers to no littles of ours," and smiled. I don't remember what we said after that if much of anything, but we left within minutes of me taking that pill. I do recall something interesting that happened after we left. He had been acting totally fine about this (almost as cold as I was now acting), but instead of turning to go back towards his house, he turned in the direction I was going to get to Jessica's boyfriend's place. He was in front of me by a few cars because I waited a minute before leaving; my stomach ached with pain over all of it.

I was in a disillusioned state of mind trying to absorb all of this because I didn't know what to hope for at this point. I couldn't even begin to comprehend the destruction that Charlie had done. The whirlwind of the last few weeks was unreal, and I never imagined I'd end up in this place. I was also scared of what the pill would do. Would it cause a worse period? Would it hurt me or make it to where I may struggle to have kids later? These were things the pharmacist probably addressed very clearly when I was zoned out paying for it.

I saw that Charlie pulled into the gas station on the corner I was about to pass. He didn't go towards the pumps or the store, though; he just did a 180 with the truck so he was facing the street, and I remember seeing his face. It was almost like he flipped the truck around to see me drive by. He looked very upset; I'd go as far as to say he looked like he may have been crying.

I won't lie, anytime I saw any emotion on his part (which was extremely rare), my head was all over the map after what had happened. Sometimes it gave me the strength to push him away because I felt like I had the upper hand. Other times, I was more calculated with my actions when opportunities presented themselves. I began to feel that if I could hurt him or make him feel small or unwanted in any regard, it would give me some justice for what he did to me. If only I knew back then how much those ways of coping would do me more harm than good. The majority of my future actions only hurt myself from this point forward.

I made him the main person in my audience for a long time after that night. Everything that I did was in some way to get his attention and to spite him for the most part. I hated him for hurting me, but most of all, I hated myself for trusting him not to. It began to feel like I deserved all the bad that came my way. I deserved it for being so stupid and for believing the best in him…for *all of it*. Highly untrue, but I still couldn't seem to shake those feelings or voices in my head.

All of the verbal abuse that my ex's family had thrown at me hit home more than ever, and I felt every ugly thing they had ever said amplified like a loudspeaker in my ears. Not just them but literally any bad thing anyone had said to me or about me. My goals became simple. *Rebel.* Being a good girl never got you far, did it? Friendless. Always taken advantage of. Always misunderstood. Alone. Humiliated. My ex's mother and aunt used to treat me like I was the sluttiest girl in the world because of my cup size. And most likely because of their actions when they were teenagers; projection is all too common for so many people. None of it had really gotten to my heart until after what Charlie did to me. I had truly known who I was (or so I thought) up until that point. It almost became like a defense mechanism to change. I didn't realize it yet, but the process of becoming a shell of myself had already begun.

Denial

I remember getting to Dave's (Jessica's boyfriend), and I was too embarrassed to wear my boots up to the door, so I brought my sneakers with me and was planning to just leave them outside. His mother was so nice and literally let me wash them off in their kitchen sink. It was there that I finally asked a couple of questions that prompted me to tell more of what happened to Jessica. I just wanted to know more about Plan B because I didn't know what to expect, and I knew that she had taken it once before with her prior boyfriend. She knew Charlie fairly well, too, and had a crush on him a couple of years before.

She and I were the only friends who would come back the following morning to help clean up after he'd throw a bonfire in high school. I remember Jessica got sweat all over the four-wheeler seat one of the mornings we came to help and because I knew she liked Charlie, so I used my t-shirt to wipe away the sweat where she'd been sitting before he noticed. I wish I could say she'd do the same for me, but sadly, I learned the hard way less than a year from this point that she was not the friend I thought she was either.

Through a series of questions about why I took Plan B and who with, she ended up wanting the details. People who knew me well knew that I didn't sleep around. I told her some of the bullet points from that night. Even from the few things I shared with her, she declared that what happened to me was rape. I remember her exact words, "Oh my God-he raped you." And I just looked at her like she was crazy and denied it. I changed the subject, and the night moved on with other things. I spent the night at her house, hoping for a distraction. I woke up the next morning and wasn't up to fulfilling my last shift at work. I had a headache (it could have been from the pill or just from all of it), and my stomach was still in shambles over trying to process everything.

My temp boss, who had literally been the sweetest person, turned on me within seconds when she heard I wasn't feeling up to coming in. I was still in bed at Jessica's when I called to make sure they had plenty of notice. She said in the rudest tone to not ever ask for a recommendation from them for future job opportunities before hanging up on me.

At first, I was upset over this because I worked my butt off every day that I came to work. I was never late and never even had many questions about how to do my job. Just showed up, got it done and went the extra mile with customers daily. But I began to not care the more I sat with it. My heart was becoming more and more hardened with the days that followed. Especially towards people. I began to only think of myself for a change, but it didn't make me feel much better. It actually took more from me to transform into someone I wasn't. But if I didn't change, I knew that I wouldn't be able to face myself in the mirror or survive the pain I was in.

While I was a mess on the inside, I kept getting up and acting like I was fine most days. I was still going to my classes and trying to uphold a believable smile at home. Not long after everything that happened, I got a call from Charlie during my English class like before. I called him back after class, but I was having a particularly bad day that ruined my ability to hide my feelings. Especially since he was speaking to me as if he hadn't wronged me in such a profound way. The emptiness that had been swallowing me whole grew to anger at that moment.

I chose to be fairly direct with him when he asked me why I was being short with him in conversation. All I recall saying in response was, "You know that what happened with us was not okay." He owned that, but the specifics were not discussed at that time. I remember later that night he asked if I could come over so we could talk about it. And I did. It was late, after 8, and I jetted out there hoping to at least hear some sort of acknowledgement of his disturbing treatment of me.

Instead, I get there, and he's in the basement on the couch playing video games. Nothing was said between us for a long time, and then finally, I said something about wanting to get going if we weren't going to talk. I don't remember him apologizing, but I do remember him trying to wrestle me, getting hyped up, putting on a motorcycle helmet, and literally crawling around on the floor like some crazy person. He had this ginormous amount of drool coming out of his mouth when he met my gaze, and I could tell for a moment he was embarrassed. I told him I was leaving and left it on semi-stagnant terms. I felt like an idiot for even coming. Things were only getting weirder and worse between us, and I started to realize that he probably wasn't capable of understanding what he had done. Hell, I didn't even want to accept what he had done, so how could he begin to?

I didn't see him again until Jamie came to get me for the movies (within two weeks of this last encounter), and he invited Charlie to join us. I started being a little clingier with Jamie, and I'll admit, I did it to see if it would bother Charlie. I wanted him to feel my intentional cold shoulder and lack of desire for his presence. Terrible friend to Jamie, I know, but like I said, I was becoming a colder version of myself in an attempt to avoid any more pain. I could tell that my bleak efforts bothered Charlie a bit, but not enough to provoke him to say anything to me.

Everyone else did what best suited them, and I felt like maybe it was time I did the same. Even if it didn't render the desired results, it would at least remove some of my vulnerability. I guess I stopped feeling guilty about Jamie's feelings when I remembered the first night we all hung out after high school for Charlie's Halloween campout; I was supposed to be his date, but he took the snorer. He had a chance…and I wasn't about to ever let a guy have the upper hand on my heart again. I began to dress a little slutty, wore darker makeup, darker everything, really. We started hanging out with Pete again, and he and I exchanged numbers.

He was living in a halfway house for drugs. Back when we were in high school, I'd never known him to have issues…he seemed like a nice enough guy. Plus, he was like 6'3 and I had a thing for tall guys. Charlie and Jamie were right around 6 feet tall, so they weren't short either. I began taking more mental notes on people's weaknesses so I could better prepare myself to hurt them before they could hurt me. I also had a newfound craving for male attention. I felt like I just needed to surround myself with more guys, talk less, and be smarter with my exposure. I didn't realize it yet, but I was basically plotting revenge against Charlie.

John joined the group not long after this. He had been in my ex's grade a year ahead of us. He had an intercom in his car and would constantly announce my embarrassing high school senior nickname (a reference to my breasts being on the larger side) through it. It didn't matter where we were, public places or not. Instead of calling that out or finding better friends, I laughed it off and frankly took pride in it for the first time in my life. I was judged one way or another for my boobs, it seemed. I wasn't even allowed to go swimming with my ex's family all throughout high school because of my figure. So why not welcome some ownership of what I'd been blessed with? I was 117 pounds at 5'7, and I had always been insecure (especially before I'd lost weight during my first breakup). I decided to say the hell with insecurity and rock what I had.

I remembered Charlie always talking about his type: tan, drives a truck and can sing. I was none of those things; I'm Sicilian and Irish, but the Irish took over my skin. However, spray tans weren't out of my reach. And a truck did end up in the picture a few months down the road from all of this after I traded my SUV in. The singing thing was not really a gift of mine, but it never used to stop me from singing in the car with Charlie on all of our adventures in the past. Cryin' on a Suitcase and Chasing Cars were the usual songs I always remember us singing on the backroads coming to and from Westwood at night. I Won't Give Up was one of the more serious ones we'd duet along with tons of others.

I think it was the lyrics we'd belt out all the time that laid thoughts in the back of my mind about us. Sillier moments also filled my car speakers when I'd blast Barbie Girl if he ever had to change from work in the back seat. So many memories that used to make me laugh and smile now made me nauseous. I had to force myself to bury the tattered remanence of all the used-to-be "good" somewhere deep within. *But bury the "good" with a smile, I told myself...you're in control now.*

My new goal in life became to not let Charlie think he ruined me or that he frankly mattered to me at all. That meant pretending to be completely indifferent. I also wanted to turn his head while putting on my show; the more I acted like I didn't care, the more he seemed to "miss" me. I knew the best way to quickly get over someone was to get involved with someone else or stay busy. I kind of did both in the span of 3 months. I just wish I had realized that I wasn't trying to get over a crush gone wrong…I was trying to get over something horrific that I hadn't even begun to process.

Unfortunately, I stayed so focused on my hollow intensions until I became just as empty as my goals. I posted a selfie of one of my first spray tans to social media; Ralph and my ex from high school got into an odd exchange on the post. Charlie made mention of this to me, and once I realized that he was paying attention to my social media, it only fueled me more to continue with the charades.

While I seemed to be fine on the outside, my family knew something was up with me. I had been ditching classes and going to the mall or just going elsewhere to hang with friends. I got a tattoo (one that is still very symbolic to me, thankfully; it was the first of many), and I started smoking cigarettes. My 4.0 GPA began to evaporate with each day during my second semester.

The spray tan thing was not like me at all, but I went weekly for several weeks to keep it up. And I'm pretty sure my parents really started seeing red flags when I began to unravel over any little thing. I even ran into the garage door late one night on my way to

Suntan City. And when I say ran into it, I ran into it on the *inside* of the garage, as in I literally didn't even open the door before attempting to pull out...*I was losing it.*

I think my mom knew. She didn't know what happened in detail, but she knew me, and she could tell something was really wrong. I remember crying before I had hit it, too; I'm not sure what triggered it, but after that happened, I just began to fall apart. Thankfully, my parents didn't make me feel bad about it because they could tell it was a total accident and something was not right with me. I remember Dad saying he had been wanting to get those replaced and get carriage doors anyway. I cherish my father's heart.

I can't help but smile when I think of my mom and dad; I am truly so grateful that God chose them to be my parents. If it hadn't been for them, I would have gone down this dark hole and likely never come out of it. They had faith in me when I had absolutely no faith in God or myself anymore. They still saw *me* through my new persona and my various shields of self-defense until I could finally see myself again, too. I truly believe with my whole heart that God places people in our lives to remind us of His Truth...that we are *beloved.*

In a world where everything is so chaotic and self-absorbed, it can be hard to hear God's whisper, but His voice is the Voice of Truth in the storms we face. We just have to be able to tune out the craziness of life long enough to hear Him. At this point in my life, I was still so consumed with self-loathing and confusion. The devil truly had such a grip on my eyes and my heart; all I saw was this broken, distorted image of myself, and I was too numb to realize what was real. Because of that ugly combination, I was not able to hear or see anything good when it came to myself. I was listening to the voices in my head, telling me that my answers for finding peace in this mess lied with Charlie somehow. That was where my focus continued to remain for a long time, and it showed. I'm just so grateful that my family never gave up on me, even when I pushed them away.

Gasoline

The day after my garage door accident, I remember there being an event at Westwood. It was some sort of activity night, and Charlie and I had been planning to go since December. I was surprised that he remembered and acted like he was still counting on going. This oddly brought back some feelings of hope; I'm not sure why I was that naïve. I still had my cold front on, casual and collected, spray-tanned and all in freaking February. It was freezing outside that night, and I only wore my ex's long-sleeved Ron Jon shirt with ripped-up jeans and vans for some reason. Knowing me at the time, it was to ensure that he saw my spray tan. I'm not sure why he drove us to WU in his truck that night, but I do remember parking at his place. Seems weird that we didn't think that through based on where Westwood was located in reference to his house versus mine.

My friend Marie was there that night, and I remembered her telling me about her troubles a few months back during our first semester. Her ex-boyfriend had raped her, and when he did, he tore something and gave her some sort of infection that landed her in the hospital. I couldn't even imagine when she told me that story, and now, here I was, seeing her again for the first time since last semester with Charlie by my side of all people. I ached to confide in her. I knew she would understand my profound confusion and sadness because, like me, she had been hurt by someone she thought she could trust. I still was nowhere near ready to call it rape, but I knew what had happened was in the same zip code. I was desperate to talk to an objective person who had experienced such a violation.

But how could I tell her what happened and then she later recall seeing him beside me that night? As much as I wanted to reach out to meet and talk over coffee about everything sometime, I knew two things…one, she may not want to talk about her trauma, and two, what a weird thing for me to be spending time with someone who put me through that. I figured it would just be another unpleasant experience for me to stomach. I had never really had much luck in finding true friends, and I figured this would be the absolute worst time to pile on any more hurt in my life.

I had been used to judgement, but I was more vulnerable at this point than I had ever been. My focus was rather singular…surviving this mess. And because I didn't know how I was going to find my way yet, the way I handled things with Charlie was still a very sensitive subject for me. I needed everything to be on my terms.

Sadly, I was afraid to lose him in my life because of the small semblance of control it gave me. I knew that telling someone what happened would have made his absence a permanent possibility. I wasn't near ready to face everything, and I was hoping that by some miracle, I wouldn't have to.

I didn't really socialize with any of the people I met at Westwood because I had spent so much time with my guy friends and never truly branched out on campus. Well, that's not entirely true; I did try…I had joined a group at school called "The Doves" hoping to make some friends. It was basically like a sorority, but Westwood didn't allow those, so it was called a "social group". Anyway, I didn't fit there either. In fact, I had a couple of girls ask me why I joined that group when I could have joined any of the other groups for 'pretty girls.'

I'll admit I noticed that a lot of the girls in this group were on the heavier side and/or quirky, but I liked their slogans and their colors, and they seemed to be the friendliest. I never thought of it as the "misfit group" but the truth was, I was *always* a misfit my entire life. Yet here I was…a misfit even in the "misfit" group. I felt like I couldn't ever find a place where I belonged outside of my friendship with my guys. And now, I was in the middle of coming to terms with the obliteration of that, too. I didn't know what I could trust anymore because I felt like I couldn't even count on myself after what happened.

It felt like I had been catapulted onto a stage where everyone who ever hated me had a front-row seat to the sad saga that was becoming my life. Memories were triggered that went beyond my ex's family's foul treatment of me; I traveled back to when we first moved here, when my loneliness first began to grow roots. During my first month in seventh grade, girls began to single me out and spit in my hair because I refused to straighten my Sicilian waves to try and blend in. I was also always made to feel ugly for my pale skin. I didn't wear makeup until I was like 16. All the while, girls were getting tans, manicures, dying their hair, and getting Victoria's Secret push-up bras at 12 years old. I just wanted to be a kid.

I had enough stuff at home that I had to take seriously, and back at that point in time, my innocence was so intact that I truly didn't care too much what others thought of me. I was lonely at times, but I was still living by Audience of One. Something I wished I had held onto for dear life during this hellish chapter, but sadly, I did not. Sadly, eventually, they all watered me down. Charlie was the final blow to the floodgates that seemed to wash away the best parts of me.

So, back to Charlie and my lack of friendships on campus…the night was becoming a bust. I didn't really know where to go, and the activities seemed fairly boring because I didn't know what we were supposed to do, where to start, who to talk to, etc. And due to the walls I was building around my heart, the last thing I was prepared to do was make myself additionally vulnerable by asking questions to learn where to go and what to do. I was too afraid to look stupid or embarrass myself in front of Charlie. I couldn't bear any more humiliation by him or in front of him. So, we left. But before we did, Charlie of course had to make a remark about how attractive he found Marie to be.

In the truck on the way home, the charades of trying to act like I was fine continued. I felt like I was caught in a melancholy moment leaving the campus with him that night; I wished I could go back in time before all of the bad happened. Back when he would come with me to chapel so I wasn't walking to my car at night alone, or just showing up to see me because he felt like it. Back when he was the friend I thought I knew. Perhaps it was the backroads we were on that took me back to that better place before the unspeakable happened.

A few minutes later, Charlie was joking about something dumb, and he began reaching over and getting handsy with me from his side of the truck. I remember accidentally spilling his drink on his pants in the commotion. We were on the backroad that was closer to the highway, and I remember laughing about what happened (it wasn't even a full drink, maybe a quarter full-mostly ice water), and he suddenly got really upset about the spillage. He yanked the truck over into some random person's driveway off the side of the road as I continued to laugh it off because I figured he had to be joking. He wasn't.

He proceeded to get out of the truck and grabbed a big red jug of gasoline out of the bed; I couldn't see what it was at first. A couple moments later he returned and poured gas all over me. It was already all over my pants and my shirt as I screamed at him to stop. I couldn't even believe he did that as I sat there soaked. After putting the jug back in the bed of the truck, he started to laugh as he bundled himself up with a jacket and gloves he had in the backseat. I didn't understand what he was doing yet.

He took off down the road, but not before rolling the windows down. I yelled at him to knock it off once I realized he was getting on the freeway and about to be going 80 mph; he didn't stop. I was freezing in the 30-degree weather, now covered in gasoline with those cold winds coming at me. He kept the windows down with the child lock setting until we got off his exit about 10 miles away.

I didn't say another word to him the rest of the way home that I can recall. When we got out of his truck, I just walked straight to mine. He seemed surprised that I was leaving and wanted me to come inside to have a dessert he had mentioned earlier. I gave a curt "no" to his invitation, got into my SUV and locked the doors. He took it upon himself to jump on the hood of my car and laughed like that was going to keep me there.

So, I started my engine, floored it forward and slammed on my brakes. Watching him fall off gave me a slight sense of satisfaction after the unbelievably horrible night I'd just had at his hands. I didn't stop to see if he was okay. I just drove around him, down onto the grass and got back on the road home.

I felt a dead end arising from that point, and that ensued a panic and an emptiness that I was not prepared to deal with. So, I didn't. At least not in a positive way. And it continued to harden and change my heart.

Looking back now, I feel like it wasn't as much that my heart changed; it was that my need to protect it with thicker armor began to overshadow what made me, *me*. I was so lost, and I knew that I needed some sort of shield to hide behind while I figured out what my next moves would be.

I should have cut off contact with Charlie then and there, but I was still too afraid to lose my false semblance of control over what had happened. I just couldn't face it. I wish so badly I could have dealt with it head on so that this ugly domino effect didn't take over my life the way it did; he didn't deserve to have that much power over me. But I guess it wasn't him as much as the devil.

The devil was able to distort my view of myself in such a way that I had to escape the sight of the truth, and all the things that used to make up who I was. A newer, harder, and stronger me had to be born to overcome the abyss of everything that I had fallen into. I just hate that my family got stuck with this stranger that I became practically overnight.

After realizing how unbelievably horrible Charlie could treat me, I longed to get away from here. His treatment shouldn't have been a shock after everything else, but again, my heart was plagued with a blindness for this reality I didn't want to face. I began fantasizing about moving away to a beach somewhere, like where all the Nicolas Sparks movies were filmed. A fresh start in a small town where the depths of the ocean could match the depths of my self-loathing. A place where I could find myself again and attempt to resurrect my happiness.

However, leaving lost its appeal in light of how close I was to my family. I knew I would never be happy without them, although, I think a part of me wanted to protect them. I didn't want them to see me in this darkness that was becoming my new normal; I carried a lot of guilt over that as well as my continuous downfall in school. My grandfather was paying my way at the time outside of a partial scholarship I had earned. And even with that incredibly generous gift, I just couldn't study or even get motivated to study. I could barely show up most days because it felt like this giant piece of me was missing. The only drive in me was based on putting on a show for Charlie and what a depressing way to live that became.

My ex from high school popped back up briefly around this time. He and I had a falling out when he heard I started dating someone within a few weeks of our split. Ironically, Charlie was the one who put an end to his texts and calls when we were on our way home from Westwood one night. I think Valentines Day was what provoked him to reach out despite the last awkward interaction we had via phone. He wanted to see me, and since I didn't have any other plans, I went.

Seeing him was hard. Not because of our past, but because of my present. When he hugged me, I wanted to cry, but I couldn't. He had bought me my favorite coffee, my favorite pizza, flowers, and a gift card for one of my favorite stores. It was very thoughtful of him, but I hesitated to accept any of it. I knew he was trying to get back together, and my heart just wasn't there anymore at all.

He took me to one of the parking lots where he had stayed before he found his rental and he put on our song from high school. He asked if I'd dance with him like we used to. As I took in the familiar smell of his cologne and the feeling of his arms around me, I leaned into him so deeply. I wanted to scream, and cry to him about everything that had happened. He had known me the longest, and we had been through so much together. But I knew he couldn't save me from this hell I was in. Nobody could. So, I just danced and held onto him for those few minutes before I left.

I think he was hurt that I no longer had those feelings for him. Our history felt so far away and foreign to me with all of the new baggage I was carrying. I was a different girl now, and the girl he once knew had basically died to herself. I felt a tug in my heart driving away from him that night; maybe because it felt like I was driving away from the old me, too. But there was just nothing left for me there anymore.

I remember my mom coming to get me from campus for these breaks on occasion when I'd be feeling extra down; we'd go for a drive or go get a coffee. She'd always show up for me like that and still does to this day. She deserved so much better from me. Honesty at a bare minimum. She was always my safe place, but after everything that happened, I just felt like I needed to face it on my own. I felt so stupid and like I was to blame for all of it. Her showing up as much as she did, even with my limited explanation as to my falling apart, got me through. And to be honest, I think she always knew more than I cared for her to.

When my mom eventually learned the details of what happened that night in January, she too went through a long period of time where she wavered in her faith. When I was a child, she prayed by my bedside every day after I would get on the bus for God to protect me, and that never changed in the years to come. I could tell when I finally told her everything that happened, a piece of her was broken, too. The guilt that I carry over that haunts me to this day. I regret that I didn't think of my family in my choices; I should have fought more for myself for their sake, if nothing else.

Jessica had called me up one afternoon and asked me if I had any plans for Spring Break. I had never gone anywhere for spring break outside of one time with my ex in high school after he had already graduated, and what a mess that was with his psycho mother. It was the only trip I was ever invited on with them, and I later regretted going against my mother's wishes; she knew it would be a disaster. The first memory that comes to mind from that trip was when my ex, his brother, and his friend and I were all sitting on the beds in the loft of the condo talking; my ex's mother came up the stairs and literally hit him in the face repetitively because I was sitting on the bed with the rest of them.

I just stood there unsure of what to do, tears filling my eyes; my ex yelled for me to leave the room. I remember crying myself to sleep that night on the back porch because I felt like there was nothing I could do to protect him. Everything always felt like it was somehow my fault because they hated me almost as much as they hated their own children. They couldn't have children of their own and went to great lengths to adopt them. I never understood why they went through all of that only to treat them with such haste and resentment. It seemed obvious to me why God didn't allow them to conceive. Had it not been an adoption outside of the states, I highly doubt they would have passed the bar.

It was the end of February when Jessica brought Spring Break up and invited me to join; the trip dates were literally just around the corner. When I asked who all was going, Jessica told me her sorority sister, Harley, and Harley's friend from her hometown,

Josie, were planning to go. They had room for one more person to split the money for this beachfront condo, which was at an amazing rate because it was a foreclosure.

I begged my parents for the 200 bucks so I could go, and they reluctantly said yes. Jessica was a student at a college just over the state border, and their Spring Break was the week before Westwood's. I should have said no just for the sake of attempting to refocus on my studies and do well on finals. I think deep down, I knew I hadn't been studying all semester or even trying to absorb stuff, so it wasn't going to make much of a difference. *I needed to get away. I needed to experience something new.* So, I took some of my exams early and some after I got back. I did fine on a couple, but Bible and Bio were a nightmare.

Prior to Spring Break, I still had a few unpleasant encounters with Charlie.

Three Bleak Nights

In the weeks leading up to Spring Break, there were three different nights where Charlie and I had moments alone together. My focus remained the same with keeping up my cold front, but I had a potential different endgame in mind. Before the gasoline night, I still had this underlying hope that somehow, if Charlie apologized to me and owned what he did, we could get past it together and go back to some sort of friendship, even if it were a distant one. As strange as it sounds, I felt like it would make the stain on my life feel smaller if we were on good terms.

If I'm honest, I was even dumb enough to still hold out hope that he had feelings for me underneath every ugly thing he was doing. I think my mind was just so desperate to believe that all of this could "go away" if Charlie would be there for me through this mess he made. At the time, I just couldn't come to grips with the fact that this wouldn't ever be something I could overlook regardless of Charlie's actions. Especially not with him continuing to treat me so poorly. He never possessed an ounce of selflessness when it came to my well-being, and that began to help me refocus on a new edge. Not exactly a healthy one, but it seemed better than pining away for someone that didn't exist.

I longed to make him feel as small and worthless as he made me feel after experiencing more hurt and humiliation at his hands.

And I figured the best way to do that was to discreetly lead him on without giving away any more of myself and then pull the rug out from under him when he was hot and heavy in the moment. I also knew that there was a chance he might try to override me again if all went according to plan, but I knew that this time, I would be ready. I felt like I could redeem myself if he tried anything like that again, and there was a small part of me that hoped he would so I could have a fresh excuse to physically hurt him. At this point, redemption through vengeance was the only light at the end of this dark tunnel that was imaginable. And believe me when I say, I imagined it often.

I was plagued with thoughts on what that would feel like daily. I found myself pondering the freedom from this horror I felt when I had to look at myself in the mirror. I wondered what he saw when he had to face himself in the mirror, too. Did he see the cruelty in his eyes? Did he know of the darkness that lived within? Or was he as free of all of it as he seemed while I remained a prisoner to January's memory?

I began to zero in on my new goals to make him vulnerable and to humiliate him. I was done being treated like I was just trash at his disposal. I discovered it wasn't going to be difficult to accomplish my goals seeing as how Charlie did most of the work for me; he created several situations where he could be alone with me to try and get intimate again. The only part that was difficult in sticking to my plan was the fact that I had this disturbing connection to him; I used to feel like such a disconnected freak because some part of me felt more whole when we were close.

I later learned that it wasn't because I longed for him but because I longed for the *pieces of me* that he took. He was this connection to the old me and parts of me that I desperately missed. I wished with my whole heart that somehow, I could just go back in time. But there was no going back. What happened, happened. And I still needed to face that...badly.

Bleak Night Number 1

There was a night that he came by, and I remember he had the GMC truck rather than his own; he said it was his favorite and his dad let him borrow it. We went out on a short drive in the neighborhood connected to mine and he parked it in front of the little park area on a tiny one-way looking road. We sat there for a while talking. I told him that I was going to the beach with Jessica and some of her friends.

After the conversation slowed down, he leaned over and kissed me. I kissed him back. After a couple of minutes, he and I ended up in the backseat. I remember him being on top of me and kissing me deeply as he started rubbing on my leggings, and I took that opportunity when I knew he was getting really into it to stop him. He had been getting very biblical lately (reading Scripture but not applying it-*clearly*), and I used that against him.

He had said he was trying to turn over a new leaf with his ways, so I reminded him of "his faith", and mine and said that we shouldn't do this. He'd agree with me, but then he'd start at me over and over again; he tried to pull my pants down several times in the midst of his lips against mine. I stopped him each time, but anger didn't arise in me like I expected it to. I again, felt like a totally messed up individual because deep down, I wanted to be touched by him. I didn't want to have sex after how he had treated me, but I still longed to feel desired after feeling so discarded.

I wanted this darkness to go away and for him to bring me healing by treating me like he cared. Delusional. Delusional. *Delusional.* I should have been repulsed; I shouldn't have even been there to begin with. But the urge for one of two things kept me going…to get my power back over my own body, and to stay close to my innocence that he had stolen from me.

Ironically, this toxic connection is what kept me getting out of bed in the morning because in the coming months, when things changed and he was no longer in my life, it felt like I had been run over by a truck. The anxiety that flooded my heart and mind was nothing short of debilitating in his absence. But there's much more that would come to pass before those days would arrive and leave me emptier than I ever imagined.

That night, when he finally got tired of fighting me, we ended up sitting on the tailgate of his truck and sharing a cigar that he had brought with him. I remember him wanting to shotgun it in an attempt to keep our lips close. I regrettably took a strange comfort in our warped closeness while simultaneously feeling like I had control over the situation. I may have kept him from getting into my pants, but I was far from in control. I was unraveling fast. And sadly, this was only the beginning of me watering myself down for a false sense of hope.

Bleak Night Number 2

I remember he had picked Pete up, and then the two of them met up with me at his parents' church. It was a massive church; the parking lot seemed endless. We left my SUV there on the corner of the lot and headed out to State. Charlie took us over to the Student Union and we grabbed some food at Panda Express on his meal card. After that, we went and hung out in this game room where they had a pool table. The two of them started playing, and I remember that I was in a bad mood, one that I couldn't hide.

I hated it too, because the last person that I wanted to see me like that was Charlie. Of all times when I'm already feeling a little on edge with my emotions, Charlie decides to drop a bomb on me…he leans down to shoot a ball into a pocket and says casually, "Hey, you remember when you said that I might hear some bad things about you through my stepmom because she knows your ex's mom…well you were right." So, of course, I perk up, and I want to know what the child abuser and the adulterer had to say about me.

Apparently, Devlin (my ex's mom) said that I was "no angel" when she was in the pickup line for their middle school-aged kids. I assume that came up because Debbie (Charlie's stepmom) told her that Charlie and I hang out all the time or perhaps it was because Devlin's family still followed me on Facebook back then and saw how close he and I were. However, it came up, and why two middle-aged women would be standing around talking about me to begin with, I'll never know. Deep down, I knew that said more about them than it did me, but I was not in a good place to remember words of truth. The lies were all so much easier to believe in my current state of mind.

I remembered that years ago, Devlin and I were on our way to a football game at the high school on a rare good day; she reached over for my hand and told me that she referred to me as "sweet angel" to all of her friends. Polar opposite of how she treated me. I've never met someone so twisted and two-faced. On the day-to-day, it was almost as if she had a jealous grudge towards me because she had a thing for her own son.

She would intentionally walk in on him all the time when he was naked and both her and her husband would force all three kids to pull their pants down for spankings with a 2x4 board whenever they were in trouble. And when I say trouble, it could have been something as ridiculous as filling up the wrong water bowl for their dog. There wasn't a day that went by that I wasn't sick to my stomach at the thought of what else was going on behind their closed doors that I wasn't privy to. I think she hated me in part for just knowing their ugly secrets. Whatever her reasons were, ninety percent of the time she treated me like the enemy behind her crooked Southern smile. I sat on my stool in the pool hall utterly pissed off that this horrible family was still able to get to me even with as far removed as I was from them at that point in time.

I remember despite my notably visible anger, I felt proud that I stuck up for myself. I'm not sure what I said, but I remember saying exactly what I felt and wanted to say in that moment regarding the pathetic matter. I also remember feeling closer to Pete that night, like a friendship might have been brewing between us. He seemed to care that I was upset by what Devlin had said about me. I could tell because he kept trying to make me laugh the remainder of the night that he was with us. And thankfully, it worked; I remember he somehow got me into a better place before the night was said and done. Apart from the anger, I was also hurt because I didn't recall Charlie saying he defended me in that conversation…he was just the messenger.

Pete had to be dropped off by a certain time that night, so we headed to his halfway house from the campus. From there, we drove back towards the church to my car. I remember smoking with Pete whenever we'd hang out (I had been doing the same with Jamie, too), and Charlie made his disapproval known when it came to cigarettes. I just remember smiling with each puff I took, thinking, you're the reason, you a**hole. He made negative remarks about my smoking on the way home that night, but I didn't justify his disapproval with a response.

I bought my first pack when I was on my way home from

classes at WCU. It was about a week after the rape. I remember I got the green pack of Marlboros; back then I used to always ask for hundreds. I sat in the parking garage after I attended a makeup chapel credit one night, and I decided to open them. I had left earlier than I should have, but I couldn't bear to hear anything out of the bible with all that was going on. I was in such a dark place and the light that came from the sermon and the songs was too bright for the shame I was carrying. It also just made me even more angry with God at that point in time; I felt like I had been robbed of all of my joy and He didn't protect me. I had begun to wallow in my darkness, and I felt like I was in uncharted territory the more I continued contact with Charlie post-rape.

He was such a self-centered monster that had hurt me beyond belief. It was no mystery that he would continue to hurt me more and more each time I allowed further exposure, and yet, I still craved his presence in my life. And I couldn't even admit that twisted truth to myself. I couldn't admit *any* of it. So, I just started doing whatever would take me to a place of nothingness…a place where I could numb away the pain and confusion even if only for a few minutes. I wish I had known that numbing myself was only going to end up heaping more pain and destruction onto my heart, but I didn't see how things could get worse at the time.

I took a few hits in the parking garage that night, which was also a big "no-no" because it was a smoke-free campus obviously. I remember the night I did that because when I got home, I went on the back deck and had a second one, but it ended up making me feel sick. I got into bed right after I came back inside. The room was spinning, just like my life.

The first time I had ever heard of Westwood, I was 14 years old, and it was my birthday. My parents had taken me there for a Steven Curtis Chapman concert. I learned that night that I had a big crush on his youngest son, who happened to be drumming for him. As I lay there in bed with my head spinning from smoking my second entire cigarette, all I could do was ponder how I got here. What kind of Christian guy would ever want to be with me now? I felt like I was a disgusting, unwanted, damaged mess. And sadly, I didn't know just how much more damage I would cause myself by not facing everything I was running from.

After we made it back to my car from dropping off Pete, Mr. 'Anti-Cigarettes' pulled out another cigar. I was surprised that this was starting to become a thing he would occasionally carry because of his chronic and open demise for smokers. Yet, it aligned with his growing pattern of hypocrisy. Perhaps he had taken on a new bad habit too…or perhaps, as I said earlier, this was some weird attempt to keep his lips close to mine.

He asked me if I wanted to join him. I accepted. The first thing I had ever smoked was a cigar with the very person who first introduced me to Charlie…my friend, Will, whom I met when my ex and I were on a break in my junior year of high school. Charlie happened to have the same strawberry-flavored one and everything. He wanted to shotgun it again like he did the previous time he had one on him. Shotgunning was typically for marijuana, so I knew this was a request with secular intentions. I wasn't near done wanting to mess with his head the way he had mine, so I went along with it.

After our lips met and exchanged smoke, he randomly started talking about how leggings drew his attention; I was wearing leggings that night. I remember him touching my leg and saying it made it difficult for him to "not want me" when I wore tight things like that. He treated the situation like we were both responsible for needing to work on keeping our relationship in the friend zone. He said I was making that challenging. I knew in my gut that this was his backdoor way of creating another situation where we would start making out in the backseat, but I wasn't in a good headspace to pretend like I was this cold-hearted, strong overcomer of all the hurt he had inflicted on me.

It had been a hard day, so I decided to avoid eye contact and not give him an open opportunity to kiss me. Charlie casually referring to our 'friendship' always caused me to cringe post-January. It brought me to this place that was all too close to reality, forcing me to see glimpses of the black hole I was entering into by treating this like it was a game. I was acutely unaware that I was forfeiting the game in my avoidance of addressing what he had done. I lost the moment I ever let his voice tell me what I was worth. It took me far too long to see that the only way you ever overcome or win at anything is when you find your value in The Voice of Truth. Everything else is fleeting and temporal; kind of like the ways I was going about handling this mess.

I had learned the hard way that Charlie and I were never the same kind of heart, and our friendship was never real. If it had been real, he would have respected me saying **NO**… and I wouldn't be in this horrible place where I couldn't stand to be alone in my own skin. This desperate place where I stooped so low as to keep him in my life to feel some semblance of control in all of it. My hate began to rise as I sat in the passenger seat momentarily reflecting on everything.

Charlie randomly started "opening up to me" about some of his sexual stuff after a couple of moments passed in silence. He talked about the last time we hung out when he brought the GMC over. He shared something rather odd with me…he said that when I wouldn't have sex with him, it caused him to shake; he assumed I noticed, and he wanted to explain it. He told me that when he wants to be with someone, he sort of "convulses", and he'll start to shake, and his stomach will even ache if he can't be with that person.

I started to remember him shaking when I wouldn't give in

to him that night, I just had no idea it was because I wouldn't have sex with him. I thought he had just been cold or something. I didn't say much, just listened mostly because I didn't know what to say to that. Truth be told, I don't really remember why he said he shakes, and I don't think he knows why he does, either. I was starting to see that he had problems that were beyond my understanding. I reflected on everything he said that night as I drove home...*what exactly was I dealing with here?*

Bleak Night Number 3

I was with him driving back near State again, but I don't remember why we were going up there exactly. It could have been to bring something to Pete or to pick him up for an outing. When we were on our way back from whatever we did, January somehow made its way into our conversation…but of course, it came up under the circumstances of sex, not rape. So, I asked him point blank, "Was it good?" He replied quickly without hesitation, "Yeah, for you just lying there it was pretty good." After a moment of silence, he started talking about how his grandfather had just passed away. I assume that this was the one who had abused him.

I'm not sure when this was exactly, but it was prior to Spring Break, likely around late February. I don't remember the specific words that led up to this, but I do recall him having to abruptly pull over into an old, abandoned gas station parking lot where he started sobbing after telling me of his grandfather's death. I was one hundred percent clueless on how to respond in this moment when I considered the screwed-up predicament I was in. The old me, the girl who thought he actually gave a s**t and was a good soul, would have been right there with a shoulder for him to cry on and probably some words of comfort, too. But this girl had been betrayed on levels that were unspeakable.

He cried awkwardly for a couple of minutes while I didn't

say a word, and eventually, he apologized and got back on the road. I pegged some minor questions about his grandfather, but he didn't elaborate. He apologized again for crying, which naturally led me to say that I was sorry I didn't know how to be there for him. He said he had hoped that I would let him lean on me and comfort him. I was quiet because deep down, he knew that I would have had he not put me through hell. If I'm honest, I didn't hate seeing him cry; seeing that he was capable of some emotion was actually kind of nice. However, I remembered learning in school that even sociopaths have the ability to cry on *their own* behalf.

I finally replied with something like, "Well, I didn't know you'd want me to comfort you." He said that I reminded him of his mom, and he felt like I was a safe place. I didn't know where to put that, so I just disassociated myself from the remainder of any serious conversation. For me, that was a way of making him feel alone in his vulnerability, but I didn't do that great of a job at even accomplishing that. I couldn't decipher what direction I was going with my somewhat 'bipolar' actions and responses.

Often times I'd just react to whatever he would throw at me, even though I didn't want him to be in the metaphorical driver's seat of everything. This roller coaster left me more confused and hurt around every bend. I just couldn't seem to fully kick him when he was down the way I had hoped to. I hated him, yet I still cared, and I honestly don't know why. Even after all he did, it was still hard for me to be cold and ugly.

While that used to make me feel like a weak person or like I was somehow just as twisted as he was, I came to realize that it wasn't a weakness at all. People often mistake kindness for weakness, and that is completely false. It's always harder to be kind to those who have hurt you, and it's always easier to let people change your heart when moments for vengeful opportunities present themselves. In this particular case, I was just so lost that I couldn't seem to make any decisions that made rational or beneficial sense for my well-being.

In my confusion, it was almost like I was trying to figure out how to respond to someone who had hurt my feelings, when in reality, this was me trying to figure out how to navigate a terrain I never should've had to climb. I did a really terrible job at keeping a straight line with my objectives because there had been so many things that I loved about Charlie, and I found it near impossible to consistently wrap my brain around his cruelties. Especially with how he continued to act like what happened with us wasn't rape…it messed with my already fogged up head significantly.

I couldn't make what he did fit into who I thought he was from the years prior to where we were now. From a far, confusion seems hard to comprehend in my situation, but when you're in it, it can be very deceptive when something like this happens at the hands of someone you loved. Truthfully, there is no place you can put it. And the fact that I wanted to burry this and run from the truth as much as possible only made me more susceptible to the severe ups and downs that come with avoidance.

The days that I did accomplish my goals of being cold towards him never made me feel stronger or better. They just made me feel even further away from myself and any form of real peace. And it sucked because the person I missed most in this messed up situation was *me*. Charlie deserved my ugliness. He frankly deserved to be behind bars for what he had done. But I deserved to be *free* from all of it; I just didn't know how to break away from the chains that had formed around me.

I hadn't told anyone at this point all that I was going through, and the omission of January's events carried a heaviness that continued to make webs around my heart and eat away at my soul daily. Jessica (who was the only person for several months to know anything) never checked up on me, and that got into my head too— like maybe this wasn't as big of a deal as it felt.

While I don't remember her ever saying anything about cutting him out of my life, reporting it or asking if I was okay, I also don't recall trying to talk to her about it. Maybe she was afraid to bring it up. In spite of all of that, I was just super grateful for the Spring Break invitation. It was a much-needed getaway for sure.

And the truth was, I still didn't want anyone to tell me what to do in this mess. I felt very strongly that I needed to find my own way in this.

A Frigid Snow Day

There was another day that my depression and anger showed in front of Charlie, but unlike previous times, I didn't try to cover it up at all. I was honest because I wanted to see if he would even care that I was clearly not okay. What a horrible letdown of a day that turned out to be. About two weeks before I left for Spring Break, Charlie invited me to hang out with him, Pete, and Pete's girlfriend at the time. We picked her up from work and went back to Charlie's house to go four-wheeling. It had been snowing, and it was freezing, so I'm not sure why we chose to do something so stupid.

We ended up all four getting on the four-wheeler somehow, which was comical at first. He tried to floor it up this big hill across the street, and we tipped it over. Thankfully, no one got hurt, but we were soaked and ready to call it at that point so we could warm up. I remember he was such a jerk and made me ride on the very front of the four-wheeler on the way back to his house. It took me right back to that night at Westwood on the way home in the frigid cold.

I know I didn't have gasoline all over me this time, and the winds weren't 80+ miles per hour, but the discomfort I was in could have reached a potentially life-threatening circumstance. I was struggling with wet, cold hands to hang onto the front bars, which were my only support. He kept flooring it and stopping abruptly, and I nearly fell off multiple times while he seemed to find pleasure in watching me struggle. It really began to piss me off and scare me that he'd (literally) put my life at risk like that. I could have cracked my head open if I had been flung off with how fast he kept jerking me. I yelled at him to stop, and he just laughed.

When we got back to his house, I took off my jacket and flannel because they were soaked and tried to warm my numb hands by the fire in his living room. I remember him looking over at me; my spray tan seemed to make my cleavage pop even more in my low-cut white tank. I knew I "looked" good, and I found confidence in that hollowed-out reasoning. He came and sat down by me on the fireplace and started talking about extending the night.

He wanted to go do a bonfire at a place I'd taken him, Jessica, and Jamie to when we were first getting close again after high school. I called it "Base," and that's sadly one of the places where my ex had to sleep when he first left home and had no other place to go. He had carved my name into the picnic table down there by the creek along with a few other words that shared his love for me. I wished he had been able to live up to the words he wrote. Maybe I wouldn't have ever ended up here I thought.

I told Charlie I would need to go home and change into some dry clothes before I could go. So, they followed me to my parent's house. I went in and changed and then we went and got firewood at the gas station on the way there. I remember Pete and his girlfriend making out in Charlie's truck for a bit while he and I were sitting by the fire alone. I couldn't help but feel so angry and depressed at the memories of us being here just a few months before…back when I was untainted by his ugliness. He asked me how I was doing and noted that I seemed different. I was honest and admitted that I wasn't doing great. He said something on the spiritual side at one point in this empty conversation that I don't really remember much of. It must have been something about praying because I recall saying, "I don't really pray anymore." And that was true.

I had felt so far from God in all of this, and I didn't have the words to pray. I felt like I fell for someone because of their Christian tactics, and all of them ended up being acts from a wolf in sheep's clothing. How could God let that happen to me? Why did Charlie and I even have to rekindle in the first place? Why did my ex let us fall apart? Why did I finally feel free of that mess and find such immense happiness, only for it to be so temporal and fleeting? I felt utterly shattered and like every attempt to pick up my broken pieces left me bleeding even more. Especially when I had to listen to the person who hurt me most in the world preach at me about praying.

The emptiness I felt was profound and whether I was with a group of people or completely by myself, it was able to hold me hostage to its darkness. I loathed myself for being in this place. I knew I was screwed up, and all of this nonsense with Charlie was only getting worse. Yet, I was unwilling to remove myself from the toxicity because I felt like pieces of me were now permanently stuck in that dark place. Pieces of me that I wasn't ready to part with yet. It's repetitive but true; I was stuck in a gear.

I could tell that Charlie knew that he was to blame for why I was in such a dark place. My responses to him were hardly subtle. It was the first time that I had been so cold without leaving any wiggle room for him to try and reach me and make it better. Mainly because all he ever did was make it worse. I was shutting down, and I was beginning to savor the flavor of my numbness. I went back and forth on letting Charlie see some of my vulnerabilities in this mess, but eventually, the walls that I put up became rather permanent for obvious reasons.

Realizing that night by the fire was another clear dead end for finding any healing, I called Jessica and made arrangements to stay at her place and left a few minutes later. Before I left, Charlie seemed disappointed; he didn't know what to say to my blatant responses combatting with his "spiritual encouragement." *Go figure*. I wondered if some part of him wished he could go back in time too. Would he do things differently? I wondered if my absence even bothered him at all or if convenience was always the ruling factor when it came to me.

Whether some part of him cared or not, it was clear that the uglier side of him always showed up one way or another when I dared to try and find out. What he needed to understand was that whether I was physically there or not, I wasn't really present anymore. He had killed a part of me…frankly, the part of me that I loved the most and yet now had such a divine hatred for. I hated that part of me because it led me astray. That part of me believed the best in people and it subjected me to more damage than I ever thought possible.

Whatever was going on in his head didn't matter anymore. I couldn't turn around. Couldn't go back to the old me. She was gone. And that realization, while existent in my head somewhere, was not at the forefront of where it should have been so I could have dealt with it properly. Yes, I had been raped, and yes, it was by someone I had fallen in love with, so it was all a giant consuming and confusing mess, but if I'd had the fortitude to see beyond the storm back then, I may have been able to save myself (and my family) from so much more pain.

I like to believe that none of us are powerful enough to destroy God's plan for our lives. I'll never know what my life would have been like if this hadn't happened to me, but I know that all I can do now is find a way to continue reminding myself of the Voice of Truth. Even when I feel a lack of peace where I so desperately crave it, I don't want to do what I did back then and for several years that followed. Running, numbing, or attempting to hide from pain doesn't work…pain demands to be felt one way or another.

While that reality is unchangeable, I've realized my answer to survival…all I have to do is *look up* and remember whose daughter I am. It doesn't always feel that simple, but living according to His truth in the midst of my storms is the only way I've ever found that's truly given me the ability to breathe again (*against all odds*). And it shouldn't end there…we don't find a cure by looking up once; it's something we must continuously do. Just as the waves of life never stop coming, we must never waiver in our efforts to stay close to God. As fragile hearts go with the human condition, we need His love and His grace *all the time*. He is the only one who can bring any real healing and clarity to our stories.

Unfortunately, I was so far from looking up at this point in my life. This was just the tip of the iceberg. I kept on doing my self-destructive dance and didn't realize just how far down I was going to fall before waking up. I think another thing that weighed on my heart was all the red flags I experienced prior to the rape. I remember he had begun grabbing my boobs randomly at times. And way before that there was the biting, and the bruises…he even whipped me with one of his belts once…why didn't I run for the hills with his weird behaviors then? I felt like such an idiot for not seeing what a strange person he was. All I can say in my defense was how these odd occurrences were always peppered in with so many good things. Things that made me happy.

In high school, the guys who started calling me my nickname

related to my breasts would occasionally spank me…I lumped a lot of their behaviors into that toxic category of "boys being boys" which I guess was a sign of bad things to come for me. Even some of my female teachers would laugh at the nick name, as did I back then. I shouldn't have, but I think it was still so surreal for me to get attention like that. After being such an outcast, to be recognized for my looks and to be considered desirable in any way felt good. I watered several jokes and things down from popular people during my junior and senior years to try and soak up what I thought was "normal." I liked not feeling invisible, even if it was at the expense of some inappropriate jokes.

I had never felt wanted outside of my high school boyfriend and look at what I endured in that relationship…?! I didn't even write the half of it in this novel.

Spring Break

Spring Break was basically here, and I remember being really excited to go but also very nervous. I had dealt with travel anxiety in the past, and I was unsure of how I'd do with being this far away from home for six days with everything that was circulating in my mind. I invited the guys over the night before we left, and the girls all stayed at my house so we could bug out early. My parents bought pizza and coke for everyone, and we got to relax and get ready for the trip. Charlie didn't come, or if he did, it was for a very short period of time because I don't remember him being there. I had gotten another spray tan and was ready to have a couple states between us at that point.

The next day, we took off somewhat early, and we all took shifts driving Harley's Honda. It was hilarious because Harley had a sister named Jessica, and Josie had a sister with my name. I remember being so pleasantly surprised that I didn't suffer from anxiety like I expected, but I did have some other symptoms that I later learned were anxiety manifesting itself into physical issues. For example, my hand was tingling off and on, and it began on that trip. I had major diarrhea twice on that trip, too; once at a frat party in a toilet that was not flushing and already had vomit in it…no bueno. Thankfully, I don't think anyone knew who did what, so I was relieved in more ways than one. I'll circle back to that party later.

When we got to the condo, it was pretty dreamy. The view was beautiful, and we had a balcony overlooking the ocean with private beach access. Jessica ended up having a lot of anxiety on our first night, so I stayed in with her while Josie and Harley went and smoked weed on the beach. We had some "Jamacinme Happy's," I believe they were called, and watched some TV. The next day, I went with Josie and Harley to get ice cream from Walmart after we had spent the day at the beach and grabbed dinner.

Jessica stayed in for the ice cream run because she was talking on the phone to Dave, who happened to be staying in Destin about an hour and a half from us. On our way back, there was a dude on a crotch rocket and a blue lifted Wrangler with a bunch of guys in it; they were trying to get our attention to ask for our number, and they were driving on the wrong side of the road to do it. It was hilarious. Somehow, we managed to write Josie's number on a large enough piece of paper, and they were able to see it and save it on one of their phones. They were frat guys, but not the typical obnoxious, J-Crew wearing type; they seemed way more laid back.

They called us and invited us to follow them to their place across the bridge for a party. One of the frat guy's parents owned the house, it sounded like. All I could picture was Natalie Holloway as I reluctantly agreed to go with them. I thought of my parents, and I felt a tremendous amount of guilt right beneath the surface…but that wasn't enough to stop me from being stupid. We let Jessica know, and she was smart and decided to stay back at the condo even though we offered to come get her. Josie hopped out and drove the Jeep for a minute, and we followed them to the house. It was in a neighborhood, so that made me feel a little better since it wasn't too isolated.

I remember there were a ton of other people at the house, including some girls. They were all surprisingly very nice. No off-color funny business was attempted, just a lot of flirting and some reciprocation to it, mainly on Harley and Josie's part. I think Josie slept with one of them, and Harley might have too at some point during the few days we spent with them. We ended up hanging out with the guys several times throughout the trip.

There was this guy, Ben, who had a huge crush on me, and his friends kept telling me he was a Catholic virgin who had been waiting for the right girl; they practically begged me to get with him. It was very odd, and I didn't have the same feelings, but I enjoyed his company. He was a nice guy. He was super tall, too, and seemed like a linebacker. He asked to take a picture with me, and then he posted it to Facebook…I remember that getting Charlie's attention.

The next day, we hung out with them at the beach, and some of them came back with us to our place and ate. We ended up showering and going back to their house the next two nights in a row and partied with them until 3 or 4 a.m. Ben's friend kept coming up to me and telling me that Ben was obsessed with me, which was beginning to make me uncomfortable. I think I did kiss him at one point, but I kissed someone different each day, which made me feel empowered. *Currently rolling my eyes as I type that, but sadly, it was true back then.* Ben was hurt, I could tell, but I decided that I didn't owe anyone anything anymore.

I made out with Rob, the president of the frat, and then this hilarious, sarcastic guy, Tony. I shot gunned beer with the rest of the guys on the porch and came in third, had a cigar, and the girls and I killed it at beer pong. We took so many hilarious photos with these people…quite literally, the most random friendships ever. And it was a blast!

At one point, Josie and Harley wanted to go down to Panama to meet up with some friends from their hometown who were partying down there. They wanted to stay the night. Jessica's boyfriend was kind of a jerk when she asked if she could stay with him and his mom on the way down as we were passing through Destin. He said no. She started to have major anxiety by the time we got to Panama, and I couldn't blame her. He had always been a heartless d**k, in my opinion, and I never for a second believed he had any real depth. Certainly not enough to be faithful.

To get into this hotel where the girls were trying to go, we literally had to be hoisted over a wall because we didn't have wristbands to get in as guests. One of their guy friends had to help all four of us get over the side of the wall that was by the McDonald's where we parked. Of all days to wear my shortest mini skirt…thankfully, I had my bikini on underneath. It was also pouring. I remember this place being a total hungover, drunk fest, and it was only the early afternoon when we got there. Jessica finally got this call from Dave saying that he had changed his mind and we could both come to stay with him and his mom in their luxury condo suite.

I went to get my shoes, and this guy, Louis, was wearing them, so I stole his shirt. Cute guy, but too short for me. Another guy grabbed my a** randomly as if he were feeling me out as a bedroom prospect. Speaking of bedrooms, when I was grabbing my stuff to leave, I walked in on Josie, rolling around naked in the sheets with one of the guys there. I didn't see who it was, but I awkwardly grabbed my stuff and left with Jessica. We had literally been there for less than twenty minutes, so I figured it was a smart choice for me to leave if the guys were expecting all of us to put out.

After we got to Daves' hotel, he and Jessica spent the majority of the night together until it was time for bed and then he had us sleep on the couch out of respect for his mom. I figured it would be just me out there. Before we went to bed, I remember Charlie calling me. I took the call on the patio alone. He sounded different. Almost like he missed me and was trying to get closer to me. I didn't know where to put that at this point, so I brushed that feeling off and kept things just matter-of-fact but upbeat. I used to have to work at this, but at this point, I wasn't having to pretend anymore. My heart had genuinely grown to a colder place when it came to him over the last few weeks in all of the "bleak nights" we spent together.

We had hardly spoken since the last time we were alone, and the separation always caused me to look at things more for what they were. *When you're too close to something, it's hard to see it for what it really is-major lesson I learned the hard way.* In addition to the boos, I'm sure that all the attention I was getting from other guys aided me in putting up a stronger defense armor as well. It was purely smoke and mirrors, but I grew to enjoy this newfound sense of control I was feeling that didn't feel as dependent on Charlie.

I described the trip when he asked me how it was going; I didn't leave out many details from some of the funny moments, like breaking into the hotel, the frat guys and how we randomly met them on the highway of all places. He asked about Ben because he had seen the picture that he posted of us on Facebook. I told him that he was a sweet guy and he had offered to take me to Formal for the group I joined (The Doves) at Westwood. While I knew I wasn't even planning on attending, Charlie immediately piped up, saying, "I would have taken you to formal!" I was shocked he said that, and it took me off guard for a moment internally.

The thought of us ever being in an actual "couple-like" situation with intention on his part was something I never thought he'd suggest. It was completely against the way he seemed to feel about me and how he treated me. The word *dude* was constantly flying out of his mouth in reference to me anytime we spoke, and as I said earlier, it cut like a knife after everything that happened. Thankfully, my response was rather quick when I told him it was the same weekend Rose had her formal that he was taking her to on the West Coast.

Rose was a fun chick and very much like me, primarily only having guy friends. We used to hang out quite a bit separately and all together in high school. She and Charlie had been very close before high school ended, and now that she was off across the country, they barely saw each other. They seemed to always be strictly friends too, but I had developed enough fake confidence to not care one way or the other.

His response regarding the timing of the dance almost sounded like he was disappointed that he had another commitment, and I remember ending the conversation shortly after. I went to sleep wondering what had just happened there…I'd never heard him sound like that before. *Now he's acting like he cares?* Even though there was this part of me that longed for him and still wished desperately that somehow all of this could just go away, I fought to remember the truth. I knew in my heart it was too late, and I needed to stay focused.

I reminded myself of the coldness and the cruelty he had no problem spewing all over me in January when I was at my most vulnerable…laying there naked in the back of his truck, literally shaking as I told him I couldn't do this…his response…*we already are.* With a smile so stealth and evil in that moment I couldn't believe what was happening to me at the hands of someone I called *friend.* He became a stranger to me in that moment, and now he had forced me to become a stranger to myself in order to survive it.

*F**k him I thought…f**k him. Don't fall for it-stay focused. Your friend is dead.*

The next morning, we took Harley's car back to Panama to pick her and Josie up and then drove all the way back to where we were staying. It was getting towards the end of the trip, and I think that was the same night we went to *The Hangout* with some of the guys. We ended up at a hotel for a few hours with some of them and their mutual friends. Harley and I took turns riding the crotch rocket with Zach, and we took some last-minute pictures with everybody. We enjoyed our view one last time as we packed up to head home shortly after.

Tony and I had snuggled up on the last night before we went back to our place. I remember he was my favorite of the three I made out with. He reeked of beer the first time we hung out during the day; it was literally coming out of his pores, but he kept me laughing with his sarcasm. Jessica made sure to stay in touch with everybody, and she and I ended up meeting up with some of them a few months later in Florida when I tagged along with her and her family for a trip. But I never saw Ben, Rob, or Tony again. They were nice guys, and I was just very grateful we didn't get raped or murdered for our poor choices in hanging out with complete strangers that whole trip.

Homecoming

I was thrilled to be home. Mom was so sweet to let me plan a get together so my friends could come over the same day; she made her homemade pizza that everyone loved. Harley and Josie had to get home, but Jessica, Jamie, Pete, John, and Charlie were all coming. Dad picked me up at the Starbucks by Jessica's house. I asked him if we could stop by Suntan City on the way home because my spray tan needed some help now that I had been using sunscreen and makeup and showering all week with it.

It looked like the blotchiest thing if I didn't get it done every 5-7 days, which was beginning to be a pain in the butt. I was so anxious to get this particular spray because I was hoping it might be more believable after coming back from the beach. I remember a single raindrop landed on my arm as we were leaving the parking lot before the color had fully soaked into my skin, and it stuck out like a sore thumb with my paleness.

When we got home, I got dressed because I couldn't shower for 24 hours with that thing. I should have cleaned up better and not worn jeans that had been in my laundry, but I really wanted to look a certain way. I had grown very particular in how I dressed and had my hair and makeup. I wore my black strapless dress from the trip when everyone arrived, mainly for when I greeted Charlie in the driveway. After a bit, I switched to my dirty jeans and one of my new ripped-up shirts I bought down south to be more comfortable. I would later regret the jeans…

When everyone first got there, we pretty much dug into the food. Jessica took pictures of Charlie and Jamie sitting on me goofing off. I was happy to have opportunities where I could easily try to pretend things were normal. I felt more whole when I was with them, and especially Charlie, for all the twisted reasons I can't explain. It's like even though I felt like I was on a dangerous cliff, the adrenaline of the 'what-if' factors kept me clinging on…like what if tonight's the night you get some unexpected healing, or what if tonight's the night you avenge yourself…those were the thoughts that were ever circling my mind. All the while, I, of course, felt the need to look my best and continue putting out a persona that reflected confidence.

After I changed, I went out onto the deck, and we took some hilarious pictures that still make me laugh to this day, if I'm honest. I remember I finally got to get this picture pose I had always wanted to do ever since I saw Beth (a family friend) doing it when she was my age on the beach. She had like four guys holding her up longways for a photo. Sure enough, I got the boys to all hold me up the same way.

I got a couple of cute pictures with Mom, too. I also vaguely remember Charlie helping my dad with something in the yard before we hung out outside. I thought that was oddly nice…seemed almost like he was trying to score points with him or something. Meanwhile, Jamie (unbeknownst to me) was in the kitchen while we were all on the deck at one point talking Mom's ear off about how he thought it was time he and I became a couple…like, literally, *what the heck was going on?* He gave me no indications that he was trying to upgrade our friendship again, and last I left it with him, nothing had changed in that regard for me.

There are two things I'll never forget from this night that were relevant to my agenda...one, Charlie seemed almost offended that I was taking pictures individually with everyone but him at one point, and I distinctly remember him saying, "We need a picture." So, we did. We got a few actually. That was very unlike him; he was not a picture person. We also got a couple of the three of us (Jamie, him, and me). The second thing I remember were the efforts Charlie ended up making to be alone with me at the end of the night.

After Jessica and Jamie left, John, Pete, Charlie, and I went out to State before taking Pete back to his halfway house. I know Pete being at a halfway house sounds so terrible, but I really didn't think anything of it at the time. He made me laugh, and he seemed like a good friend who was trying to get his life back on track, so I was always happy to include him.

We hung around the Student Union for a bit, and I remember

Pete picking me up and cradling me as he spun me around. It was the first time we had ever flirted outside of our usual sarcastic banter. On the way to and from State, I remember Charlie sitting in the back with me intentionally, even when the front seat was available. He put his head on my lap and wrapped his arms around my waist; I could feel him breathing deeply as I began to run my fingers through his hair. I'm not sure why I did that, but he seemed to like it. Before Charlie laid his head down on me, I had been dancing and singing along to all of these songs from Spring Break. It was clear that I was able to find happiness in spite of everything, and I was grateful to showcase that in front of him.

Jamie had been making ugly jokes at my expense earlier on the deck that night after I had been on his shoulders for a picture, to which I was completely oblivious at first. When I later learned what he was saying and why, I was really taken back. My pants, as I had said before, were something I'd later regret. They had been in the laundry when I grabbed them, but they were my favorite, and I really wanted to feel confident, so I wore them even though they were technically dirty.

Jamie kept calling me "captain," which I guess was code for me smelling "fishy" down there. It was very hurtful when I later learned that he was being crude about my hygiene while simultaneously sweet-talking my mom about us dating within the same 30 minutes. Super weird and screwed up, just like everything else. This is something I would have corrected had I known, but I was more focused on my looks than taking care of myself the way I should have back then.

Apparently, whatever I smelled like didn't bother Charlie at all. In fact, it seemed to almost turn him on the way he kept his face near my crotch the whole time we were on the drive home. He had mentioned something about going to the woods and having a late-night bonfire. John caught wind of that and said he was all in. And this is where it gets interesting…

Charlie did not want John to come. He wanted me and him to be alone. I had a feeling that was the case because after he realized John was trying to come, he suddenly acted like he needed to head home. John was bummed but acted understanding. As we pulled into my driveway, Charlie got out with me, and I remember him continuing to say he was going to head home as he said bye to John and even to me. As we stood there watching John pull out, I could tell he was full of it.

John wasn't even all the way out of the driveway before Charlie looked at me and said, "So, you ready?" And I played the part. I told him he was so bad for saying that to John, but deep down, I was glad he did. I wanted to be alone with him, too. I wanted to see what he'd do with an opportunity like this. I know there had been some opportunities in the past 3 months, and I handled them okay, but I felt like I would be even better now with my inflated ego from the trip.

Although Spring Break did provide a lot of cloud 9 moments, I still felt like a hollow shell of myself beneath my fake tan and smile; I was just getting better than ever at not letting it show. My confidence was all an act solely based on the wrong things, and I just desperately hoped no one could see through it. Especially Charlie.

Insanity

As we drove to the woods, I wondered what would come of this night. Would this be the night where I'd end up having to fight him off and avenge myself? Would he tell me he was sorry and own what he had done? Or would he profess feelings he had been hiding from me? I didn't know what to expect with how clingy he was being since the trip. I think if I'm honest, I still (deep down) hoped he would ask me to be his and that I could somehow bury what happened between us and just be with him.

I've never admitted that…not even to myself until now. But the truth was, I still was battling feelings for him for whatever warped reasons existed between my heart and the notion that he had one. And I wanted him to want me in ways that would bring me healing, not more pain.

One thing I knew for sure…he was not going to get to have me this time. Even if he were to be vulnerable and admit he wanted me to be his girl, I knew I couldn't let him have his way with me. But even with sex being off the table, I wanted to be intimate. And I knew he did too. So, I let it happen. I was ready to take back what was mine if he were to be the monster he had been to me before. I just hoped it wouldn't come to that.

Sadly, even if my deepest desires of avoidance were to avail, it never would have made right what he did. No matter how he went about the night or anything in our future, it wouldn't undo what he took from me. The damage was done. And if I would have woken up from this ridiculous cat and mouse game back then, my wounds would have found reprieve a lot sooner.

I was still so confused by everything and stuck in my own fog that I just couldn't see the better path to take at that point. All I knew was simple…I wanted some form of peace and healing no matter what it looked like to someone else. Unfortunately, my security was primarily based on him showing desire for me, and that in itself would never be enough to change anything for the better. I needed to see myself through a lens that reflected value again, regardless of his treatment of me. I just didn't know how.

He drove us out to the same area where it had happened months before. His insensitivity made me wonder if he was choosing to be oblivious to the painful memory or if he did this with intention. I looked out at the field in front of us, into the woods where my innocence was stolen and where I lost myself. I had this contorted vision of it as we sat there in silence.

My need to fill that gap was blocked off with so many feelings; a combination of numbness and pain struck me as I came face to face with the field. After his parking choice, I had alternative thoughts on how to respond at this moment. I thought about breaking the silence with the truth and seeing what he would do with it.

However, my desire to call him out on everything in a more direct way than I had attempted before was tamed by his usual small talk.

He began asking me questions, mostly about my Spring Break and this dance coming up. He asked me about the guys I was with and things that I don't really remember fully. And then it began. He leaned over the armrest and started kissing me. My heart throbbed out of relief, feeling his lips against mine once again. (Unbelievably wrong, I know. Believe me, I feel so disgusted even writing this sad truth out.) I thought that maybe out of his strange jealousy from my Spring Break stories, he'd put himself out there and really talk to me.

Truthfully, I had hoped for some profound apology to swoop in and save my heart from this endless torment. I didn't know what words could overcome such horrific actions, but I prayed they would come anyway…followed by being held. *So crazy and dumb…I know*. He had made it clear that he was beyond incapable of doing anything *remotely* close to what I was hoping for. I just knew that he held my missing pieces, so I felt like I needed him to be the one to fix me.

Idiot. The voice in my head was never shy in telling me how dumb I was choosing to be, but at the time it didn't feel like a choice. It felt like the only way.

As the kissing continued, he wrapped his arms around me,

pulling me closer. I remember trying to maintain my focus on what had to be done if he were to cross the line. Minutes passed like this, and he never paused to share anything real or admit any remorse about everything with us. I was afraid to be dumber than I already had been with this guy…it began to feel like before…just another opportunistic make-out session that he hoped would lead to something else…sex that I would maybe not protest and just lay there for *again* in his mind.

So, sadly, even though he wasn't leaning towards the direction I was hoping he'd take this, I was turning my gaze to the only other pleasure I could take in this moment…making him feel unwanted. I sucked at that, though, because deep down, I did want him. But I wanted a version of him that didn't exist. I wanted him to make it right somehow. I didn't know another path to redemption outside of finding healing with him or hurting him back. I didn't understand that there was a third option; I could have chosen to get my life back on track. I wish I had taken that road instead, but back then, it truly felt impossible. I didn't even know where to begin.

As we started to make out more intensely, he shifted gears. He pulled away from me and got out of the truck. I didn't know what he was doing at first until he came around to my side and opened my door. He reached in, picked me up, and carried me to the back seat. My fear began to arise, mixed with the screwed-up and distorted pleasure of the moment. Mainly a fear that I'd have to fight him off.

There's nothing more uncomfortable than being vulnerable with someone in such an intimate way and then having to be prepared for them to treat you as if you're worthless. And there's nothing more confusing to the heart than experiencing that type of whiplash with someone you thought had a love for you…at a bare minimum, a respect for you that wouldn't dare compute with their own selfish desires.

I had learned that Charlie wasn't capable of such feelings before, but of course, in my damaged heart and mind, I felt like it was somehow because of *me*. Me not being pretty enough. Not being more enticing. Not being as alluring as I should have been. You name it, and I thought it. I just thought it all beneath the surface of this new persona I had been working so hard to put out there. This stronger, sexier, more confident version of myself that was "immune" to Charlie's ugliness. But for those who truly loved me and knew me, it was plain as day that none of that was the real me. I wish I could go back and tell myself that I was enough just the way I was before.

I'm sorry, Mama. I'm sorry I didn't tell you. And I'm sorry for the dark path I chose to cope with this mess and how badly that hurt you. I'm sorry, Dad, for choosing every possible bad choice after you chose to be such an amazing father and example of what I should have held out for. I'm sorry I threw myself away...I'm especially sorry I threw myself away over this person. And most of all, I'm sorry I chose to run away from my Audience of One.

There, in the backseat, we were making out like before. Flashbacks kept entering my mind, forcing me to take a mental grip on reality. The fun was gone. He was trying to undo my pants and, in fact, did before dragging me across the back seat of his truck. He dragged me across the backseat several times, trying to get them all the way off after I told him no repeatedly. I said this wasn't right and that we should stop as I kept having to pull my pants back up. I continued as I had in recent weeks, using Christian morals as my reasoning. Considering he was still acting like he was "close to God," I figured it was worth highlighting that these actions didn't adhere to the lifestyle he claimed he wanted. It worked for a few moments; he'd stop after taking in what I said, but then he'd go right back to fighting me again. Nothing had changed.

Finally, after a fourth or fifth time occurred when he was struggling to pull my pants off, I flat out told him that sex was not going to happen. He didn't so much as skip a beat when he curtly said, "You really think it would be like that again?!" I was taken back by how quickly this blunt side of him appeared in the midst of feeling rejected. I don't remember my exact words in response to that, but I said something along the lines of "Yes, I do.". He had given me no reason to think otherwise with his aggressive and seemingly singular desire to get into my pants.

Once he realized that I wasn't going to let him have me in that way, he gave up. I know we had been in a similar situation a month or so prior to this night after we parked on the side street in the GMC. However, I think being back in the same location as the rape brought me to reality all the more quickly with how stupid I was being. Plus, the blunt and cold behavior he displayed after feeling rejected was like a dagger to my open wounds.

This ridiculous plan to make him feel small didn't help me *at all* like I'd hoped it would; I felt even emptier not long after the night was over because I knew deep down that putting myself in that position again had been such an *insane* decision. I use the word insane because the very definition of insanity is doing *the same thing over and over,* expecting a different result. Clearly, there was never going to be a different result, at least not in the way I was going about it. He showed no remorse or care in the world to try and repair any of the damage he had done. I didn't matter to him, and I felt dumb for misreading his jealous moments as terms of endearment. *Healing would not come from him.*

His frustrated attitude with me continued as we got back into the front seats. I had perfected my coldness and acted like I was in control of the situation and good with it. The truth was, the more I realized how he was continuing to only seek me for sex, the more that grew to be true. Even at my worst, I knew I had much more to offer than just physical pleasure. There's a part of me looking back that wishes I would have taken the opportunity to just punch him in the face the way he deserved in those moments where he continued to try and get me down to my underwear again.

I had every right to, and perhaps it would have made me feel less pathetic in the long run, but I didn't. I was also glad to shed some light on the smoke and mirrors he was putting out there with the so-called "faith" he hid behind verbally and musically. Using it against him felt good. As much as I wasn't in a good place with God after what happened in January, I still couldn't stand people who hid behind bits and pieces of the bible for their own twisted agendas.

Through this mess and several others, I learned to never fully count on people to be true representations of God's love for us. We are all imperfect, and we all suck in a multitude of ways because we are naturally selfish-it's the human condition. I hate that throughout so much of my life, I felt unworthy of God because other people made me feel as though my mistakes and shortcomings were tattooed on my forehead. I'm sure that a lot of people experience that. Now more than ever, I strive to remember that *God is good, and His love is pure. He does not reject me.* His love is not of this world because it's unconditional, something that can be hard to fully grasp in this life. We don't deserve what Jesus did for us, but He did it anyway.

We can't earn our way to heaven. All we can do is choose to accept the beautiful gift that He chose to give us, and that is *His grace*. He gave us the free will to choose. And even in our walk with the Lord, we will fall away, mess up, and fail…but He never leaves us. I lost my faith in all of that truth during this dark time I was walking through in my life. It took me a long time to *look up* and embrace this beautiful story I used to read growing up. We had it on a plaque in our home. It's called "Footprints in the Sand," and it rings so true for all of us in one way or another:

One night, I dreamed I was walking along the beach with the Lord. Scenes from my life flashed across the sky. In each, I noticed footprints in the sand. Sometimes, there were two sets of footprints; other times, there was only one.

During the low periods of my life, I could see only one set of footprints, so I said, "You promised me, Lord, that you would walk with me always. Why, when I have needed you most, have you not been there for me?"

The Lord replied, "The times when you have seen only one set of footprints, my child is when I carried you."

On the way home that night, he asked me again if I really

thought what happened in January would happen again. I didn't know what to make of that. What happened in January…what did *he think* happened in January, I wondered? His irritability showed in his tone, and the way he was driving the truck was making his anger at the situation fairly transparent. We hadn't reached the pavement yet when he asked me this. Did he fully understand the magnitude of what took place in January? It seemed obvious that he did not, but I wondered if he internally took some ownership that he had forced himself on me.

I responded vaguely and decided not to get into it now that I realized nothing had changed in him; he was still simply trying to have sex with me and nothing more. And I felt like without pleasure in the mix of possibilities in his mind, he may choose to be even more cutting with his words…I had seen how cruel he could be on a whim. Sadly, I was just so mentally depleted that I couldn't bear to try and address the reality of what he'd done when it came down to it. Weak, I know.

I just kept thinking, stay in control, don't show emotion…and in order to talk about what happened (especially since I still was struggling to call it rape and I was buried in self-blame over it), I'd have to get into every aspect of my emotions. No, I thought…the safest bet was to stick to my guns and not elaborate. Let him simply feel unwanted, not desirable enough…let him think that I was above him, calling the shots, and wiser for holding true to "our" beliefs.

With me at least feeling some sense of control over my own body again and some control over his pleasure when it came to me, I thought I'd be able to rest in some relief for a while. After how he acted, I wanted to discretely make him feel small and keep him at arms distance. I was still afraid to part ways completely for all of my stupid reasons.

To top off the night, he showed more of his true colors before dropping me off. He said that when he can't "finish" with someone he's gotten that hot and heavy with, he usually has to get with someone else right away. I guess this was his way of trying to persuade me to come onto him out of fear that he'd get with someone else…more proof that he never really knew me. I've always had way too much pride for that type of nonsense.

Unfortunately, he fulfilled his statement a couple weeks later, and he did so with a fifteen-year-old girl when she was high as a kite. It would be three more months before I would learn of this disgusting situation. I still carry guilt over that to this day. Perhaps if I had said something back when this first happened, he wouldn't have had the chance.

Collide

A couple of weeks later, Josie and Harley returned to town and wanted to hang out. Jessica was unable to join them that weekend, so they stayed with me at my parent's place (sort of). We didn't really stay there either because we ended up staying out all night with the guys before crashing at a house through one of Pete's mutual friends.

First, we dressed up and went to the big mall in the city to meet Charlie, Jamie, Pete, and John. Unfortunately, the mall was closed except for the theater and Dave n Busters. Consequently, we ended up wandering around, dressed up for no particular reason, and goofing off for a while.

Pete then invited us to accompany him back to where he was staying North of the city; the area wasn't exactly what you'd call 'safe'. It turned out he had left the halfway house and resumed drinking. I didn't know much about his past, nor did I feel comfortable passing judgment or attempting to intervene, as I was dealing with enough of my own issues. So, I just went along with it.

He said that we could have drinks at his friend's house, where he was staying, and that we were welcome to spend the night. Since we were going there anyway to drop him off, and the girls and I happened to have spare clothes in my car, we decided to accept his invitation and stay.

The house was clearly a party house… I'd go as far as to say it was an amateur crack house. I later learned that Pete had been into crack and all kinds of drugs, not just weed and alcohol. But at the time, I wasn't even thinking about my well-being in those regards; it was simply about continuing to save face and pretending like I was fine when I wasn't.

After the recent "intimacy" that Charlie and I shared a few nights' prior, the emptiness that followed left me anxious to prove myself. I had hoped that the feelings of being in control of that situation would be lasting; I wanted to persevere beyond the vulnerability that was still seemingly stamped across my forehead. Sadly, nothing felt better internally for me at all. More proof that everything I was doing wasn't helping my situation. If anything, it was only making all of it worse by keeping him in my life. Trying to prove myself to *him* was never the answer.

We got dressed in our sweats and whatever we had brought in the car to sleep in. I hope I had the decency to at least tell my parents we were safe that night. I had begun to disappear more and more. Even when I was home, I wasn't really home. My mind was so focused on other things, everywhere but where it should have been. Processing the reality I didn't want to accept. I felt like I wasn't even me anymore. This other persona I had taken on began to be the only version of myself I desired to be because the stupidity of my old self became such a point contention for me. *Why didn't I just fight harder? Why didn't I see this side of him?*

I hated myself for being in this position. This position where no matter what I did at this point, I felt so screwed over…literally. Why did I have zero confidence…why couldn't I just accept that Charlie was a horrible, horrible human being and move on with my life? None of this was me anymore…and everything that I loved about our friendship had been destroyed. The innocent and carefree times we had until 2 in the morning were now being replaced with alcohol, drug houses, and empty intimacy. I just wanted to wake up from this nightmare, but I began to drink instead. It became my easy escape…an escape that came with so many other problems. It's like the commercials for any type of medication…while this numbed my pain temporarily, the list of side effects was long and tumultuous.

I remember everyone snuggled up to someone and found a place to sleep in the crammed room we stayed in that night. I don't remember Charlie staying there long, and I'm pretty sure he didn't spend the night. I think he left because he had work the next morning. I remember Pete unexpectedly cuddling up to me on the tiniest photon. Him being 6'3 made that rather difficult and kind of amusing.

The next morning, Jamie, the girls, and I were all getting

ready to head out. I remember Jamie pulling my pants down in front of whoever was in the room as we were about to leave; I was wearing my lime green thong which I'm sure made that moment even harder to miss. I was pissed that he did weird things like that sometimes, and yet, I never fully addressed that like I should have out of self-respect.

On the way home, Jamie and I sat in the back seat and when I put my hair up, he said something else that rubbed me the wrong way. I remember him saying, "Huh…you actually look really good with your hair up." Almost as if to say, "I didn't think your face was pretty, I'm surprised…"

I don't remember anything from during the day, but I do remember that evening. Pete still had some personal items at the halfway house, and we all piled into my SUV to go pick his stuff up. If I'm remembering right, I believe I ended up getting into Harley's car with her and Josie, and the boys drove my SUV back to Charlie's house. We followed behind and were planning to stay the night.

Harley and Josie were going to have to leave early in the morning from there, so that's likely why we drove separately; that and the need for more space for all of us. We had decided to do a late-night bonfire in the woods and had bought everything we needed on the way over. How great, I thought to myself. I was worried that I wouldn't be able to hide my emotions…how the heck was being back there, with him going to work? I knew it wouldn't be hard on him to continue to act like nothing ever happened because clearly in his mind, what he had done wasn't a big deal. All the while, I was drowning in all of it. The good, the bad, the ugly, and now more of the unknown.

I needed a favor. I was scared to undergo more pain, so I remember asking the girls when we pulled into his driveway for backup. Since John, Jamie, and Pete were all there too, I asked them if they didn't mind blowing Charlie off if he were to make any passes at them. I told them he had done me wrong recently and that we were not on the best of terms.

The girls instantly replied saying they had my back and had no problem icing him out if needed. I was grateful to them for that because they agreed to this without even knowing the details whatsoever. At that time, I hoped to be able to avoid divulging anything about that mess. Plus, the small bit I did share was true—he had just done me wrong, again—and we weren't on good terms. We hadn't spoken much since the woods, and I was becoming increasingly uncomfortable with the unknowns of which side of him I was going to end up around in these social settings.

Earlier in the evening when we were buying wood at the gas station, I could tell Charlie was still mad because he was being short with me. Little did he know, I was upset with him for reasons that far surpassed his unwarranted frustrations. I just hoped that beneath the surface of his wounded pride, he understood that what he had done to me was wrong. I had nothing fundamental to base that hope on, but nonetheless, I did.

I wondered if part of why he wanted to have consensual sex with me was so he could feel like the first situation wasn't rape. I figured it would help him feel like he could gloss over it with more ease and a clearer conscience. Despite that disturbing presumption, somewhere deep down, I also felt like he had a genuine attraction to me at the same time.

God only knows…all I know is that I was grateful that I didn't succumb to those twisted moments of temptation when we briefly shared intimacy. If I had caved, I feared he would have gained a warped peace about what happened in January, and he would have likely lost interest in me entirely. I was mostly afraid that if that were to come to fruition, I'd unravel completely because I'd lose all semblance of feeling in control all over again.

The devil had me right where he wanted me…thinking I was in control, when really I was just surrendering to his plans for destruction in my life by continuing to try and hold onto this mess.

Even with the staggering list of reasons to abort my plans to keep smiling through this disastrous charade, I regrettably pushed forward into the abyss. I suppose I continued down this path partially because I felt like I would hate myself even more if I were to deviate from my embellished, well disguised pride and dignity; I felt as though that was all I had left. With what little temporary satisfaction I ever got out of doing things my way, I wish I could understand why I chose to stick with that plan as long as I did. Truth is, I'll never know why I chose to keep subjecting myself to such madness.

I guess it's just more evidence that rape really does distort your view of yourself and what matters. In my mind, I felt like I was waging a war on Charlie to get my pieces back, but really, I was waging a war against myself and losing more of who I was with each passing day. I felt ruined from the inside out, but contrary to what I felt back then, I wasn't damaged beyond repair. Discarded, maybe. But not by the One who matters most.

When we arrived in the woods, we ended up in the middle of this island part of the creek, and we built a fire on it. Thankfully it was in a different part than where Charlie and I had been before. We had some Arbor Mist wine that the girls had brought, and we all kept passing it around. It was a pretty awesome fire considering it was on this elevated section of the creek bed. It was beautiful being surrounded by all of the trees and the creek simultaneously.

Charlie brought his guitar and was clearly trying to serenade anyone interested, but the girls paid him no attention. Josie and I took it a step further by singing over him, completely out of tune, as he was trying to sing "Collide". We were laughing with each line and reaching out for each other dramatically, holding onto each other's hands. I could tell that he was getting frustrated that we kept singing so loudly that we were drowning out his attempts to keep the melody and focus on him.

We were a little tipsy and couldn't help but add some wine-filled charisma to the song. We were laughing so hard we cried. There was a ladder there too, leaning up against the tree, and I remember that coming up in some drunken recollection of that night for months to come. This was the beginning of what became a very close friendship with Josie for a while.

It was obvious that Charlie was beginning to get irritable that he might end up sleeping alone, and I couldn't help but smile on the inside. *How does it feel* was all I kept thinking. I knew that this was yet another mild experience of feeling undesired that held no water in comparison to the disturbing ways he treated me, but it still brought me some momentary satisfaction.

Pete came up by me and made an announcement to all of us regarding his level of intoxication, "Guys, I swear I'm so drunk, I can't feel a thing right now." I remember getting squared up with him and I smiled as I said, "Really?" right as I slapped him across the face. He moved his head back, then squared up with mine after the blow as he looked down and me…, "Bit*h." He was grinning, so I knew he found it as hilarious as everybody else did. Even Charlie laughed in that moment.

I was so grateful that I was becoming such a master at hiding what a shell I had become on the inside. I looked like I was having the time of my life. The laughter and sarcasm were the only things I could hold onto on nights like that. Some of those memories still make me laugh to this day despite the sadness surrounding them.

When we got back to Charlie's house, we were all in the basement but this time we didn't bring anything to sleep in. That or we were just too lazy to go get our stuff out of Harley's car. Charlie went upstairs and grabbed the girls and me gym shorts and hoodies. Josie and I wall-twerked in the bathroom after we got dressed and entertained everybody for a minute.

I remember Harley got with Jamie (in the bathroom), and then slept with him on the couch. Josie snuggled up with John and they slept on another part of the couch. And Pete semi cuddled up to me on the far end of the couch. Charlie was completely alone on the floor. And again, I felt relieved that he was having to face feelings of being unwanted. This was the mildest form of the bed he had made for himself, and he deserved to wallow in it.

The following morning, the girls got up and left pretty quickly. I remember thinking that I'd chill with the guys for a while and play some video games or watch a movie before helping clean up. But to my dismay, Charlie asked me to leave. It was as if he was so butt-hurt by the night before and being all alone or that he blamed me… I wasn't sure, but either way, it hurt me to the point where I can remember crying as I walked down the grass to my car.

His dogs were chasing me and one of them managed to pull his shorts I was wearing down a bit, which startled me. I had hoped no one got flashed. I felt ugly enough as it was. I had looked in the mirror shortly before gathering my things to leave, spray tan still intact, hair done, and my makeup decent for having slept on it. I had done all I could to "look the part" he always said he wanted, and yet it didn't matter. The show I put on was worthless. I still wasn't enough. Even after going to these lengths I felt more powerless than ever. In a fight, it always takes so much more energy out of someone to swing and miss than it does to swing and hit; I was growing tired of swinging and getting nowhere. I wish that I had understood I was swinging at the wrong target.

Why couldn't he bring any healing to me by at least treating me decently? How could I have misread his heart by so many miles in the beginning…did he even have a heart? I wondered why everything had to be so messed up. I felt so defeated after feeling so high the night before. The lyrics of "Unbeautiful" filled my mind and my speakers as I drove home.

NINETEEN UNSAID

More Beautiful You

I had gone from thinking I found a forever friendship or maybe something even more to this horrific dead end that left me in shambles. When he dismissed me, I felt like the ball was back in his court again and I had no leverage. In spite of everything I had transformed into to protect myself, I was more shattered than ever, because now, I didn't even have *me.* I had this tattered reminisce of the old me with shields of all things typical now impeaching what remained of my innocence.

My mouth had become so foul, my thoughts, and my desires were self-indulgent and empty. I began to have flashbacks of so many things. Some of which, I wish I could have forgotten, and some that I longed to relive. One memory that always brought tears to my eyes was this voicemail I had on my phone from my mom during my freshman year of high school. I used to listen to it often when I was feeling so picked apart by my ex's family. She called me right after dropping me off at school and said that the song "More Beautiful You" came on during her ride home. She said in a tearful voice, "That's just really what I think of you, and I hope you know that." It has always meant everything to me that she has been able *see me* no matter what storm I'm in; she's the reason I've never fully given up. And she is truly my one and only best friend in the entire world.

There are several lines in that song that haunted me during this time of my life more than ever:

So turn around you're not too far

To back away to who you are

To change your path, go another way

It's not too late, you can be saved

If you feel depressed with past regrets

The shameful nights hope to forget

Can disappear, they can all be washed away.

By the one who's strong, can right your wrongs

Can rid your fears, dry all your tears

And change the way you look at this big world

He will take your dark distorted view

And with His light, He will show you the truth

And again you'll see through the eyes of a little girl.

That there could never be a more beautiful you

Don't buy the lies, disguises and hoops, they make you jump through

You were made to fill a purpose that only you could do

So there could never be a more beautiful you

There could never be a more beautiful you <3

Even just typing that out has me crying to this day. Those words always struck a deep chord in my heart, and I could still feel them even in the midst of my numbness and pain. However, it wasn't enough to pull me back yet. I remained in that dark place for quite a long time and things definitely got a lot worse before they got better because I chose to keep Charlie in the audience of my heart.

I chose to listen to the louder voices rather than the Voice of Truth. And all those other screaming voices were winning because they had me so focused on my looks, my vulnerabilities, and my regrets. After Charlie used my body and discarded me like I was trash, all I could see when I looked at myself was an undesirable mess. Quite literally the opposite of how God truly sees us. But, as I said earlier, I ran from God because I felt so incredibly angry at all of it; I felt like He abandoned me when I needed Him most.

The reality of who Charlie was became inescapable. And the realization that he likely never cared about me in any regard filled my heart and my mind the more I thought on all of it. Maybe he wasn't even capable of that. Who knew…certainly not me. How could I have fallen for someone who could treat me with such ugliness time and time again? What was wrong with me? I wasn't this girl…this desperate girl. This girl changing herself for a guy. Especially for such a horrible one at that.

For whatever reason, I just couldn't seem to escape this mental trap I was in, and some of my old bad habits began to creep in now that I felt plagued with the reality of it all.

I had gone through a small bout with anorexia during my breakup in high school, but that didn't last long, and it was partly because of my ex's family too. They had made me feel so bad about myself, but I never expected to lose so much weight from the stress of all of that. I began to look at myself in the mirror every day for long stretches of time, analyzing my legs and if they were touching, etc. My pants were a size 2 and falling off; zeros ended up being baggy on me at one point, and yet, every day, there I was…starring and analyzing myself. Finding a small ounce of comfort if the number on the scale was somehow less than it was earlier that day.

I had finally gotten to a better place when I was free of my high school relationship and the parasites that accompanied my mind…or so I thought. Rekindling with Charlie and Jamie had truly made me happier than I had ever been and the last thing I thought about was the scale, or any other measure to take against myself. I actually consciously stopped weighing myself because I didn't want that to dictate how I saw myself anymore. The obsession seemed to just naturally slip away from me with how happy I was in my new chapter.

I wish that would have lasted. Better yet, I wish I hadn't been dependent on anyone else to feel valuable. I didn't go back to a direct battle with anorexia, but the obsession of studying my flaws and analyzing my body became a freshly sharpened knife that cut me on a daily basis after January.

After Charlie kicked me out that last morning, I never went to his house again. I cried on the way home, but then I began focusing on finding new ways to bury the pain. I knew that I couldn't count on him to show up in any way for me at this point…clearly, he wasn't ever going to be capable of bringing me any sort of healing. In fact, just the opposite kept happening at every opportunity that I allowed him near me. And trying to play 'cold and confident' never left me in a good place either.

I know this is not shocking news and most people would think I'm a complete idiot for ever letting him near me again or thinking I could gain any sort of peace from my rapist. All I can say for that seemingly fair assessment from afar is you can't move on from something until you've at least begun to accept it. And while I was beginning to see things more for what they were, the water still remained very muddy due to the combination of my self-blame and continued involvement with him.

I always had a strange sense of comfort knowing that he was still "around" even with how horrible he was. I wasn't ready to deal with the idea of him being completely absent from my life, but I certainly was done planning anything to intentionally involve him after the way he basically threw me out. I was still struggling to find a path that would leave me feeling like I had the upper hand on him. What I didn't realize was, I already did have the upper hand in every category. I just couldn't see it at the time.

Jamie was only home on weekends from school at that point, so that left Pete and John. Jessica didn't frequently come home from her school on weekends. I began offering to take Pete to AA meetings and would meet up to chill and smoke with him. The first night we did that alone, we sat on the roof of my car and had a couple cigarettes. He made me laugh and got my mind off of everything and I enjoyed his company.

A couple of weeks later, we became intimate. I don't remember our first kiss or anything, but I do remember the first night I stayed with him. He had left the second halfway house and was staying at the amateur crack house we had crashed at a few weeks prior. I didn't know much about addiction, and I was in a place where I didn't really care about others around me. I was focused on meeting my needs.

I figured that if I had been that way all along, I wouldn't be in the dark place I was in now. I had been hurt in youth groups in the past, and I felt like at this point, I didn't want to try going back to church (which is what I should have done). I wanted to be around 'friends' that were in the same boat as me…miserable. And you know what they say about being miserable…misery loves company. The last thing I wanted to do was deal with all I was running from and everyone I spent time with seemed to feel the same way about their own baggage.

Now that I had turned away from God more than I ever had in my life, I was ready to obliterate anything left of the old me. The good girl that was dumb enough to let someone as awful as Charlie run her heart over with a truck needed to go. And truthfully, I still carried guilt because I knew if I really had been such a "good girl" I wouldn't have been in that predicament with Charlie in his truck that night in January in the first place.

In some ways I guess I felt like I deserved it. Knowing I didn't put up much of a fight ate away at me. So much for 8 years of MMA. I could have taken him. And maybe if I had screamed or hit him or even tried to fight him beyond pushing him off me and verbally asking him to stop, things may have gone differently. But I froze when he ignored me. I was done being frozen. And I was done being ignored. I needed to accept that this was my new reality. And

I began to drink in efforts to absorb all the things I couldn't change.

Bad Blood and Wild Turkey

Charlie showed up the night I was staying with Pete at the amateur crack house by myself, and I don't remember why. I had this huge bruise on half of my lower arm from attempting to donate blood at school. The nursing/med students were in training and were the ones performing the blood draws, hence the disastrous bruising. After all that, they didn't even end up using the blood they did get because they couldn't re-enter the needle after 15 tries to get the last half of the supply they needed. So, they tossed it.

Anyway, when Charlie got out of the truck, he seemed happy to see me, and I remember him hugging me which was not ever a normal thing for us; I honestly don't remember us ever hugging except maybe the first time we saw each other post high school. Shortly after he drew back, he noticed my arm and his eyes widened as he held it up under the light. He immediately looked at Pete like he had tried to get me on drugs and seemed all protective for a second until I explained what happened. *Weird.*

Another weird protective moment that Charlie had that night occurred when Pete randomly picked me up in the cradle position. I remember Charlie spanking me and giving me this look like, "What are you doing?" And I just looked at him as if to say, "What? And why do you care?" Pete's friend we were staying with had a creepy uncle that was also staying there that night; he kept hitting on me and I could throw up remembering that I took a swig of Wild Turkey off his bottle. I was being an idiot, likely to prove to Charlie that I was no longer the same girl anymore. I wanted him to try and save me, I guess. Given his history, I should have realized there was no point in clinging to that false hope.

I slept on a mattress with Pete in the same room we were all dog piled in a few weeks earlier. Charlie stayed the night and got up really early to go to work before the sun was even up all the way. I felt some relief that he stayed that long considering there was nothing in it for him; it seemed like he stayed to make sure I was okay. Yet, I was still hurt that he could leave me there at all. He had to know that I was only in a place so disgusting and dark because of him.

I wish I had someone (a real friend) who would have literally just taken me out of there and knocked some sense into me, but I was still so tuned out of what was real.

Pete and Charlie both seemed to be wary of the nasty uncle. I remember Pete saying that was why he wanted me to sleep beside him in case he tried to come onto me in the middle of the night. I snuggled up to Pete for the first time in a different way. I was beginning to like him. I remember I was starting to wish he would kiss me. I knew I'd never initiate it, so if it was going to happen, he'd have to do it. I was kind of always that way before Charlie and certainly after. I maintained this sarcastic cold front while trying to appear alluring and confident even though I felt very ugly and insecure right beneath it all.

That was the last time that I saw Charlie socially for a very, very long time. So much would ensue from this point forward…some of it so embarrassing that it's unpleasant to even be repeating.

I wound up in a very toxic relationship with Pete after we began to grow closer. I remember him staying in my car at one point because he got kicked out of his friend's place and had nowhere else to go. His parents wouldn't let him come home, and he was drinking and smoking weed, so he couldn't go back to any of the halfway houses he had been at previously. I discovered that he had been abusive in his prior long-term relationship after he became physically and emotionally abusive to me as well. My life was just becoming a s**t sandwich without the bread at the hands of my ridiculous choices.

Shelter from the Storm

What got me on this fast track to sh*t with Pete was the night that I stayed with him overnight in the Walmart parking lot (gross and dumb) during a tornado. (If you're still reading this, you must be thinking 'Wow, what a winner she was' LOL). I felt like it was an adventure. As mentioned earlier, I was craving distractions, even if they were utterly absurd.

I could hardly stand to be on campus anymore because everything reminded me of Charlie and the old me. The me that I missed and simultaneously hated. And I was failing two of my classes because I had stopped trying in school altogether. Pete had actually been coming with me to some of them because he played the "protective role" and didn't want me going places alone. I didn't object and in fact invited him most days, which was helpful in creating some new memories.

But it didn't take long for him to become a new source of destruction that I'd later resent. Shocker…*the drug addict with an abusive reputation didn't make your life better??* Ughh just typing some of this stuff makes me want to go back in time so I can slap myself in the face and scream 'WAKE UP!!!!!' Needless to say, I was clearly asleep at the wheel in my life.

Pete ended up being the first person that I really told about

Charlie. I didn't even name names at first, which helped me not leave out many details. I told him the night we stayed in the Walmart parking lot. We had just been talking about random things we'd both been through, and some part of me felt like I could finally say it out loud. Frankly, I *needed* to say it out loud. It had been suffocating me for nearly 6 months.

Pete prompted me with the basic question… "Why are you doing this?" Even he knew what a loser he was, and he saw that I still had things going for me, so my choosing to spend time with him under such circumstances didn't add up. As the storm continued to get louder surrounding us in the parking lot, I felt the words assembling themselves in my mind, ready to finally leave my mouth.

I began to tell him what happened in January; I was relieved to just say it. Especially because by the time I finally said the whole thing, I called it rape for the first time. I remember him holding me, and oddly enough, I somehow found a semblance of comfort with him, lying there in the back of my car in a storm. Because for me, the biggest storm was still within.

I remember him getting high on some cough medicine and falling asleep with me.

We began to get closer and after a couple of weeks, I slept with him. Something I had never done before at random, especially not with someone I wasn't even really dating. Someone who had literally not one thing going for him outside of being the only person I shared my secret with.

His family had begun to let him back around, partly because of me, I think. They were curious. I remember them even asking me what I was doing with him. It made me sad that he had wrecked his life so much, but I was in such a disconnected place at this point. All I cared about was feeling wanted, and in my everlasting state of delusion, his possessive behavior made me feel like he really cared about me.

Things didn't stay peachy with him for very long for obvious reasons, but I didn't run for the hills right away like I should have. *Nothing new there.* He began checking my phone and being extremely paranoid about me seeing or talking to Jamie or just any guys in general. He would literally stalk me if I tried to get space from him. And one might ask how that was possible if he didn't have a car…I thought the same thing when he'd somehow show up where I was at random. He'd call John or loser friends to come give him a ride and follow me around.

He was oddly manipulative even though he didn't have anything to offer, and he certainly wasn't intimidating even with his height towering over me. I only grew close to him when I wanted to be held or have sex and that wasn't super frequent with how controlling and weird he became. He was usually the one initiating all of that and if I wanted to, I would. This was partly about control for me, but this was even more so about my self-loathing when I look back on it. I truly hated myself and I was so broken over everything…I was just letting my life continue to fall apart.

I remember the first time he grabbed my neck and slammed me up against the truck seat. It was so random and out of nowhere, and I cursed him out, but I didn't do much else. That wasn't the first time, and he would often yell at me, grab my arm, etc. And when I had moments of clarity where I would actually try to separate myself from him, he'd threaten me with the one thing that he knew would cut me the deepest. He'd say he was going to call Charlie and get him to come pick him up and say he was going to talk smack about me and stuff along those lines. Just plain ugliness basically.

Cold Exposure

Pete figured out that it was Charlie who had raped me a few weeks after I told him about what happened. He randomly asked me if it was Charlie who did it. I was surprised that he guessed, but I was honest. And then I wanted to know why he assumed it was Charlie. He shared with me that he and Charlie had been invited to house-sit with these two girls back in March. The girls were friends of Pete's, and he knew that Charlie had been with one of the girls that night. She was 15.

A cold chill surged through my body as I remembered the last night that Charlie and I had been intimate together... I remembered the gross statement that he made about needing to get with someone else because I wouldn't put out. I was speechless and I felt a tremendous amount of guilt. I'm sure he would have taken that opportunity regardless, but perhaps if I had reported what he did back in January, he wouldn't have had the chance.

Pete wanted to reach out to this girl to see if she was okay and I asked him to please not disclose my name or anything in his reasoning for reaching out to her. He claimed he would honor that, but I know that he failed to keep my name hidden in that conversation because somehow through the grapevine, Charlie became aware of what I shared with Pete. The girl said that she remembered the night being a bit of a blur because she was so high, but she confirmed that she and Charlie slept together.

The fact that she didn't remember much of the night made my stomach churn with the unknowns; her being fifteen shed enough disturbing light on the whole thing as it was. I remember drinking with Pete and trying to avoid the topic. Word got around to Jamie somehow about this whole thing as well, and he demanded to see me in person that very night.

Pete was jealous of Jamie, and frankly anybody, because he was so insecure and controlling. He was with me when I got the call from Jamie and expected to be present for the conversation. I didn't object to that…I figured some moral support might be nice. Pete and I had been parking when I got the call in a neighborhood attached to my parents that hadn't been developed yet; we agreed to meet in my driveway. I could tell from the tone of Jamie's voice on the phone that he was upset, but I couldn't tell if it was on my behalf or on behalf of himself; either way, it was obvious that he knew something about January.

He pulled up and got into the passenger side while Pete sat in the back, listening to everything. Jamie was fairly quiet at first, and I noticed that it looked like he had been crying. I asked him what was going on. He said that he had just come from Sonic where some girls were talking with him and Charlie; apparently, they told Charlie that I said he raped me. Charlie outright denied it and countered by saying that we had consensual sex. Jamie said that he left Sonic immediately after hearing this because he wanted to hear what I had to say about it.

I could tell when I started to explain to him what happened that his sadness, and even the two tears that I saw fall, were not on my behalf, but rather his. He clearly felt like I just randomly went and had sex with Charlie even after hearing my side of everything, and that hurt me on tremendous levels. He either didn't believe me or didn't understand the magnitude of the violation I had experienced. His demeanor revealed jealousy rather than anger for what happened to me.

I couldn't believe that he was that selfish in that moment… he had not an ounce of care for me or frustration at Charlie on my behalf. I was internally stunned, and my need to be cradled in numbness took over by the end of this conversation. I felt like I had just lost another friend that I thought I'd be close to forever.

After Jamie's exit, I immediately drove us back to the spot where we had been parking and had sex with Pete. He was just relieved that Jamie would be out of my life because for whatever strange reasoning, he saw Jamie as a threat. It seemed like I was just surrounded by twisted and warped people at that time in my life.

The truth was, I could have stopped it all right there (frankly any time) and fought for better, but I guess I had lost hope in finding better. All the friendships and memories that I loved and trusted had become this distorted Picasso painting. And now this horrific night was out there for others to pick at and smear even more.

I was so angry with Charlie for smearing lies about me publicly. If he was going to deny what happened, he should have denied ALL of it, so he didn't make me sound like I just slept around. And I was angry with Pete. He tried to act like he didn't name names, but I knew he was the only one that could have because he was the only person I had ever told everything to. Jessica knew, but when I dismissed her titling it rape, she never brought it up again; plus, she didn't know the girls who spoke to Charlie and Jamie that night.

It's not like I expected Charlie to admit that he raped me to a bunch of people questioning him about it at random, but for him to say the word "consensual" really enraged me. I didn't know what to do. I just knew that Jamie was only thinking of himself in this equation, just like Charlie. *Just like everybody.* It made me want to have it out with Charlie, but I didn't know how I'd go about that at this point, so I just stayed in my new bubble with Pete.

I guess you could say that I used Pete just as much as he used me…but the abusive garbage he began to inflict on me was not what I had in mind when I chose to become exclusively intimate with him. Even in my self-loathing, I didn't desire to be abused further. I just wanted an escape from my pain, my thoughts, and the voice in my head that kept telling me to turn around and go back home.

I just couldn't listen to that voice because I knew I couldn't really go home anymore…home would be different now because I would have to face everything for what it was. And if I were to accept and call things what they were, then what? Would I press charges? There was no proof, only hearsay, and even with proof, I knew it would still not likely go in my favor.

Did I even want to press charges? I still had so much self-blame with this whole thing for allowing it to go as far as it did before saying no and trying to push him off of me. And how would I explain the times I saw him after the rape? I had him in my home like nothing was wrong to save face and to try to resurrect my dignity in some unrealistic masquerade. I'd even made out with him two times post the rape for crying out loud…who would dare to try and interpret that craziness for what it really was? It felt like my desperate and frankly, terrible attempts to survive this had burned so many bridges already.

Not long after the talk with Jamie, things progressively got worse with Pete…shocker. He began to be more and more hateful and ugly with me if I couldn't meet his unending needs to feel wanted, and desired and like he was the only guy in the world. I didn't see or speak to anyone but him and my parents, and yet, he treated me like I was constantly going to cut him out of my life every five seconds.

Obviously, that would have been the right thing to do, but I let this go on for almost three months. He had absolutely nothing going for him. He wouldn't even attempt to get a job because he was so paranoid that I'd cheat on him if he wasn't right with me every second of the day. I began trying to distance myself, but he knew the code to my car, and he'd just be waiting for me there regularly.

I remember I tried to break up with him twice. The first time we broke up, he showed up at the grocery store where I was shopping within 30 minutes of our breakup call and sweet-talked me. The second time was at his parent's house in their driveway; we had a fight, broke up, and then he chased my truck before I made it out of the driveway all the way.

I was a sucker because I was scared to be alone with my own thoughts for too long; he still provided a distraction even if it was a crappy one. I do remember being so tired of his presence one afternoon that I offered him 40 bucks to go hang out with some of his friends while I hung out with my mom. The key was to make him think it was his idea. I drove him to his friend's place about 45 minutes away and literally felt such utter relief after I left him there. I figured he'd use the money to buy weed and get high enough to just stay there for the night. I prayed it was far enough away that he wouldn't be able to easily get a ride back.

Charlie never tried to call me or attempt to set the record straight from his side of things, and I think that's because he knew the truth. That or he was just scared that I might be gearing up to press charges against him. There was nothing to "set straight" outside of him owning it and attempting to make it right to my face. It was the least he could do, and frankly the only step in a good direction he could have taken at that point. However, I knew that he wouldn't own it after how horrible he had treated me in the months that followed what he did.

If he were going to try and show any signs of remorse, he would have during the many opportunities that I stupidly and regrettably gave him. The only thing I gained in that lapse in judgement was the knowledge that the goodness I'd once seen in Charlie was just a figment of my imagination.

Run

I had another two-day break from Pete when he had a 48-hour sentence he needed to serve in jail for a prior charge he had with drugs. He was down to the wire on fulfilling that, and if he would have neglected to follow through, he would have been arrested and placed in jail for a whole year.

I kept trying to get him to go, and he refused so many times on the notion that he thought Jamie would try to get with me. It's hard to even type this sad saga, in all honesty. It wrecks my heart that I allowed these types of people to ever dictate how I felt about myself, but I was truly in a place where I felt like if I were alone with my thoughts for too long, I'd consider suicide.

I needed a distraction, even if it was from the bottom of the barrel. He eventually did his time within the timeframe he was allotted, and I'm pretty sure his parents let him come home for chunks of time around that month. I remember us hanging out at their house and even going to their lake house once.

I also remember being surprised that Pete was such a screw-up because his parents genuinely seemed like good people. Kind of like me at that point in time. I carried so much guilt with all the secrets I was withholding from my family, but I couldn't bear to tell them how bad things were. They had done so much for me my whole life, and they deserved better than this girl who was just giving up on everything because she couldn't face January.

The last night Pete and I were together, he was staying at this guy's house in the neighborhood attached to my parents. His name was Dirk, and he had been one of the biggest nerds in school, but a very nice guy. I used to take up for him in high school and tell him that one day he would be the CEO of some company and all these jerks that bullied him would be working for him. When I caught wind that Pete was pegging him for a place to stay, asking him for money, and drinking his parents' alcohol, I got on him about it, but not enough.

I should have removed myself from the situation completely, but instead, I took advantage right along with him. I was nice, but that didn't make it okay. I knew that what Pete was doing was wrong and total usury. I regret being a part of that in any way. I partook in drinking with them, and I did "air duster", or whatever it's called. When Pete took me upstairs to their guest bedroom to have sex, I felt guilty, and I couldn't get into it. That pissed him off so much that he threw me off the bed.

I remember for once, I decided to leave and not put up with his behavior any longer. I went and tried to find my purse. He found it before me and threw it at the wall by my face. I just picked it up and left.

Even though he was such a pathetic loser, I was still scared.

I had been drinking a little, and I felt like I wasn't thinking straight because I was still wanting the distraction of him in my life for my lame reasons. But I knew enough was enough. I had gone too far down this dark rabbit hole, and it was time to come up for air.

I remember my legs feeling shaky as I walked out the front door and down the lawn. My parents' house was several blocks away, but I knew I would get there eventually. My instinct was to hide from him. I didn't want him to follow me and try to convince me to come back. Within ten seconds, he was running after me outside.

I began to run from him a little, and he chased me and grabbed my arm, telling me to knock it off in his condescending *you know you're not going anywhere* attitude. Some part of me was utterly amazed that this guy had the confidence he had…it was truly astonishing.

I remember him apologizing and saying some things about how much he loved me and that he wouldn't treat me like that going forward. I finally stood up for myself and told him that I was done with him, and this time I meant it. I told him that I couldn't do this anymore.

Instead of getting physical, he begged me on his knees to stay with him. When that didn't work, and I told him I needed to go home, he pulled the Charlie card. He threatened to call him and tell him things I had said when I was vulnerable and threatened to have him come pick him up.

I began to cry. I knew that Charlie hated me more than ever now, and the thought of them talking trash about me sexually or whatever else made me cringe.

I don't remember everything that I said, but I remember saying some of the things I knew he wanted to hear in hopes of him letting me go home without giving me any further grief. I couldn't bear any more of my trauma being thrown in my face, especially not from the very person that I confided in about it.

Somehow, I convinced him to let me go home, and we ended up in Dirk's car. He sat in the back with me while Dirk drove us to my house. Pete let me leave without giving me any more threats, but I remember he said he would be right down the street if I wanted to come back. He also said that he would drive by to check on me…

I was so numb and yet so distraught with everything my life had become. I was unable to cover up my tears when I walked in; my parents were right there in the living room. It's kind of a blur, but I remember I started to tell Mom the truth about Pete and how bad things were with him. She was appalled and, of course, told me that he was no longer welcome in their home and wanted him out of my life. They had been trying to convince me not to see him the entire time we were "together", so I'm sure they were relieved that

I was finally ready to cut ties.

Shortly thereafter, he began calling me. He was trying to sink his claws into me again. He regretted letting me go home. I grew angry and began to tell him off. I was tired of all of it. I told him that we were done, and then he got really angry because he knew that I played him in order to make him let me go. It was as if a small part of me were coming back to life again as I finally started to stand up for myself.

He was yelling and cursing so loud that Mom could hear every word he said even though it wasn't on speaker. She was on the edge of my bed and reached for me to hand her the phone. It was laughable to hear his responses when she called him out on how he had treated me; he denied it and just kept saying how much he loved me and garbage on that note.

She addressed him in such a way that made him unravel on a level I had never seen when she cut him off and told him what a pathetic little boy he was with his nonsense. She didn't skip a beat when she threatened to call the police if he ever so much as blinked in my direction again.

"I am a MAN!!!" he screamed back at her. She laughed and hung up on him while he was still screaming about what she had said.

My dad said he saw him drive by in Dirk's car a couple of

times, and apparently, so did my neighbor, whom he had previously dated and abused. The police were called the next morning when he continued to drive by, not by us, but by Susan's mother. We learned this after Susan's mom decided to contact my mother about all of it.

Cops

That was an extremely awkward experience, to say the least. We ended up going over to Susan's house to meet with the police there, and each gave our individual reports.

Upon walking in the front door, I immediately remember mouthing the words "I'm sorry" to her because I felt so embarrassed and awful for inadvertently bringing this jerk back into her life. She mouthed the words "It's okay," and by the looks of her body language, she seemed to sincerely mean that.

After I gave my report and Susan did the same, I was asked to step outside with the police because they wanted to ask me if I had been drinking the night before with the incidents that occurred at Dirk's house. I was honest and said that I did have some alcohol while I was there. I left out the huffing air part.

They were surprisingly kind in their response to my honesty and, of course, told me not to drink until I was legal. One of the officers also gave me his card in case I ever needed to reach him directly.

I learned a lot about Pete's behavioral history and how awful he had treated Susan in the past. I am aware that there are always three sides to every story, but based on how he treated me, I could decipher at this point that he was an unstable prick with a long history of using cruelty as a tactic in achieving his selfish desires.

Susan's mom wanted her and me to have a friendship emerge from this mess. My mom made it abundantly clear (I love her so much) that she would be comfortable with that only if our relationship was not solely based on Pete and his nonsense.

My mom did not care for how Tandy (Susan's mom) explained that she knew Pete and I had been seeing each other for several weeks because she had a secret Facebook account that she used to spy on him. She said, and I quote, "I was just glad he was leaving Susan alone."

This, of course, gave my mom cause for frustration that Tandy intentionally chose not to warn my mom or dad about Pete's abusive behavioral history.

Additionally, my mom noted that Pete was clearly still an obsession in their household and, frankly, always had been based on past discussions they'd had at neighborhood meetings. Tandy seemed to try and keep the past abuse alive by fixating so much of their present on Pete. It was unhealthy.

Mom remembered that when we were in high school, Tandy told her at a Christmas party one night about how Susan could never be away from Pete with the school zone change. I was grandfathered in, but Susan was two grades below me and Pete. In addition to fighting the school on her continued enrollment, they also opted to have Pete in as many of her classes as possible because according to her mom, Susan needed him to get through the day.

After the abuse finally came out, they tried to take it to court but waited too long, and the judge ruled in Pete's favor due to statute of limitations and a lack of evidence.

Considering all of that, you would think that they would have hated Pete, but on the contrary, Tandy acted as though they still thought highly of him. She made remarks to my mother, stating that he was a handsome and smart young man who was just really good at being manipulative. Which is probably why Tandy seemed to take offense when mom was very open about what a horrible and idiotic waste of space Pete was. Mom even asked the cops in front of them how it works with an intruder coming onto a person's property. She asked if she were to take him out on their front lawn, would she have to drag the body into the house for it to be considered 'self-defense'?

I thought it was hilarious, and the cops seemed to take it in good humor as well, even though they still provided the legal answers to her questions. Tandy did not find it humorous at all. My mom had shared a similar statement with Tandy earlier on the phone that morning, and Tandy's response was, "Susan would be absolutely devastated if something ever happened to Pete." Even though, just the sight of Pete earlier that morning left Susan in a state of horror. She was in her closet with a knife afraid for her life according to her mother just hours before we filed the reports.

My mom was still hung up on the fact that Pete put his hands on me and could've cared less about anyone but me in her rage over that. She is truly my best friend, and I am so grateful I finally let her start looking out for me again.

I really liked Susan, but I could tell that my mom was probably right; if we were to have grown close, our friendship would have most likely circulated around our sad past experiences…at least for a while. She wanted me to move on from this as quickly as possible. Pete was a stupid hiccup in my life, and she didn't want him to even be recollected as someone worth discussing.

My mom could tell from her conversations with Tandy that it was the opposite in their household. Pete wasn't just a past chapter; he was their whole story-both past and present. I had witnessed Tandy continuing to try and hold onto all of it when she proclaimed to the cops multiple times, "Clearly, Pete is still obsessed with Susan." It was as if she was afraid that I was somehow going to take that spot in Pete's messed up head. I held no desire to be Pete's obsession, but it seemed like they really valued that title as Mom had sensed.

In light of that, I took Mom's advice and didn't try to get very close to Susan. The whole situation was awkward, and I felt bad for putting my family in such an embarrassing predicament. It seemed like the least I could do at this point was listen to my Mom's intuition and steer clear of more drama. I am glad to say that Susan and I always remained on friendly terms. And from what I can tell, she seems to have made a beautiful life for herself reaching far beyond her scars from Pete.

Pitiful Awakening

When we got back to the house after the reports were finished, it was the beginning of me finally having to come out of my coma and face the reality of my lonely, screwed-up situation. And I hated it.

The following weeks began to eat away at my soul as I had no more distractions to keep me asleep at the wheel. Charlie was gone. Pete was gone. Jamie was in and out, but I limited my exposure to him because of how he had hurt me when the truth came out. I went out with him occasionally just to get out of the house, but deep down, I never felt like I could let my guard down fully around him again.

I had my first panic attack in July when I was on my way to stay the weekend with Josie. I got to take my dad's new truck, which was exhilarating on so many levels. I always felt like I was being watched, and even though I know that's not true…it gave me a rush to blare my music and drive in such a way that I achieved an adrenaline rush. Having a V8 felt incredible…I had always wanted to drive loud, and my lead foot made that happen every time I had the pleasure of driving that gorgeous beauty.

The panic attacks became more frequent and more debilitating. I remember drinking heavily at Josie's during my first episode to try and get past it; it lifted a lot of the initial weight off of me.

I was smoking cigarettes a lot more; Josie was also a smoker, so I felt like I was in good company to keep that habit going. As much as Pete made me feel worse, I still missed his presence at times because he had ways of making me laugh. He was also a male distraction. There was something about having attention from guys that I craved more than ever after Charlie.

I missed being touched and feeling desired. I felt like I was no longer in control again because of the panic attacks, so alcohol started to become my vice more and more. Thankfully, I never became addicted to cigarettes, but I enjoyed being able to have those handy for a momentary escape, too.

I also made the decision to not go back to Westwood during that time, and man, do I regret that to this day.

In the weeks that followed, my parents forced me to go to therapy. I remember that I had started to finally tell my mom what happened, and I think, in some ways, while the floor fell out from beneath her, she also found some relief in learning that I wasn't just going off the rails at random.

They had me reach out to my prior psychology professor from Westwood, who had seemed like a friendly enough guy. His office was in the city. In class, I recalled him wanting all of us to write a paper about who we really were, and he had given all sorts of examples to encourage us that he was a safe place to share our secrets. He said he even had people come out of the closet to him in these papers in the past. He talked a lot about sex, specifically orgasms and how women often times really struggle to have them. I remember him talking about a couple he counseled that had been married for 25 years, and the wife said she had never experienced an orgasm.

Several interesting topics were discussed during his class, and I figured if I was going to talk to someone, at least he was a familiar face, and he certainly wasn't going to shock easily. He was the third person that I told in full what had happened on January 10th that year. And his exact response after I finished saying everything was, "You were raped."

I was very quiet at first and then began to stutter in my effort to take responsibility, stating that I let it go too far, and tried to explain how I froze up. He cut me off by putting his hand up and abruptly called it rape once more.

I had told my mom the majority of what happened but there were some details I left out. And eventually I told my dad what happened too. I had to offer them some truth after the chaos of Pete. They had contemplated kicking me out at one point when I was still with him, and I couldn't blame them. They thought I had lost it.

I think it was safe to say that I had, in fact, lost it at that point in time. I told them bullet points, and now, I was finally verbalizing some of the details I had been avoiding in my mind for six months to this guy. I'll call my ex-professor 'Sid.' Sid ended up not being the safe place that I'd hoped he'd be. In fact, he said several ugly remarks that did a lot of damage to my already fragile psyche at that point.

He, of course, asked me if I had reported what happened. I told him I did not. He proceeded to tell me that if this happened to anyone else, it was my fault for not reporting it. I was silent. The guilt I felt for the 15-year-old girl I found out about was horrendous; now, I couldn't help but wonder how many others there were or would be in the future. Then he told me that he was appalled that my dad didn't go kick Charlie's a** and said that if he were my dad, he would have killed him.

First off, I have the most incredible parents in the entire world. My mother is my best friend, my angel, and the only one in this world who truly sees nearly every part of me and loves me no matter what. My father is my hero and has always been my safe place to fall. He has shown me from day one how I deserve to be treated and there's never a day that goes by where he doesn't refer to me as "beautiful girl".

But how could they possibly know how to handle a mess that I was so entangled in when I had only shared bits and pieces?! I had been protecting Charlie with what I chose to share because I ultimately did not want him to be permanently out of my life when all of that first happened. None of this was on my parents whatsoever. All of this was on me and on Charlie.

I blamed myself more because I was continuing to let myself fall apart, which, by in stretch, affected my parents very much. They sacrificed so much for me my whole life; they never held any of it against me…and this was what I let myself become? My education? My heart? My everything… I was a disaster. And I learned pretty quickly that Sid was the last guy on the planet that was going to be able to help me navigate through all of this in a positive way.

He continued to ask me questions, and I answered them. At one point, I shared what went on with Pete. He asked me if I had sex with him. I told him that I did. His response was… "Can I give you some advice? Close your legs."

I began to shrink in my chair, feeling more and more defeated with each session. I think I only went to five. He wanted to meet my mom and asked if she would come to a session, and she agreed. He was kinder then, but even Mom thought he was odd.

And I'll never forget on our way out of that session, in the waiting room, Ellen was on TV, and he muttered, "What a waste of skin." I couldn't believe it. The very guy telling all of us in class that he was a safe space if we wanted to share our sexuality, our story, our anything, was saying such an ugly lie about one of the biggest-hearted people out there.

He was a poser and a fool. The more I got to know him, I realized there was no reflection of Jesus in this man's heart, and I resented the fact that he acted like he was a believer. Even with how little faith I felt at that point, that pissed me off.

I remember him saying some of the weirdest things to me when I told him about my anxiety issues. He, of course, wanted to prescribe me medications right away for depression and anxiety. I declined. Then he asked me if I ever Kegel. I didn't know what that was, so he began to explain and describe it to me. He asked me to practice in front of him. Just writing this makes me want to come out of my skin. That son of a bit*h was a twisted piece of s**t.

He said that I should clench all of my muscles and do my Kegel exercises anytime I had anxiety coming on. Then he started saying things about how I deserve a nice guy, someone who would treat me with love and respect. He referenced his son and said I'm the kind of girl he hopes his son will bring home one day.

After making me feel like I was aiding in the rape of other girls, a whore for having sex with Pete, and asking me to clench my vaginal muscles in front of him, he dropped that left-field commentary on me. I knew it was time to wrap this up.

I got into a wreck on the way home from that last session. I was on the freeway and a spider had distracted me when it was crawling around in the center console. I think deep down I knew that wasn't the only distraction I was facing that day. Thankfully, no one was hurt, and the guy I hit was really nice. No damage to his truck, but sadly, I did about $3,500 worth of damage to Dad's new truck. That was the end of me farting around that summer.

I got a job at a vet clinic as a kennel technician to begin trying to pay it off. We had my grandfather's car ever since he stopped driving about two years before. I began driving that for the first few weeks and then Dad and I went and bought me an old Honda Civic. It had a hole in the door, and I didn't care.

I remembered Beth driving an old black Honda Civic when I was a kid, and it always smelled like her perfume, "Light Blue". I missed my childhood. I also didn't feel like I deserved anything nice or good anymore. And Mom saw right through my decision in that willing purchase. She fought my Dad on it, and I felt bad because Dad was just taking me at face value.

I stopped going to see Sid before I started my job, but I later regretted not trying to find another therapist. I needed therapy, and I should have forced myself to find someone else.

The Ugly Truth

Not long after I started my job at the clinic, I began seeing Jamie more frequently. On the weekends that he was home from school, we would go out to the movies or dinners to catch up. It was a much-needed distraction from my chronic depression and anxiety. It also provided me with some connection to the old me, which seemed to carry the effects of a double-edged sword at times.

Jamie felt like this bridge to moments I missed, and the temporary laughs we shared always left me aching to go back and do everything differently. I covered up the hurt that he had caused me when he first learned of the rape because I felt like I needed those fleeting nights to escape all that I couldn't change. I also decided to give him the benefit of the doubt when I thought about how odd it must have seemed that I allowed Charlie to stay in my life as long as I did.

I think it's hard for people to recognize the difference between "date rape" versus being raped by a random stranger. Date rape is done by someone you know and, frankly, someone you trust, and those two factors make it utterly confusing. To be raped by a complete stranger is just as horrifying, of course, so please don't misunderstand me when I say this.

I just think that the mind-twisting destruction that happens with "date rape" is something that a lot of people don't understand.

You blame yourself on unspeakable levels when it's by someone you thought cared about you; it causes you to question your judgement, and it can erode at your ability to trust anyone at all. Even yourself.

Additionally, I think the toxicity can overtake you if you go into denial like I did. In my case, I continued allowing that person around in false hope for him to somehow bring healing or for things to go back to "normal" again because I didn't want to accept what happened.

I'm sure there are lots of people out there who didn't allow their date rape situation to obliterate as many opportunities as I did, and I'm sure there are situations where people lost even more. Everyone is wired differently, and no case is the same.

My awareness of how many landmines our traumas can cause when they're not dealt with has grown tremendously over the years as I've looked back on all of my experiences. I came to understand that there is no "right" way to deal with anything like this.

It's a common misconception to look back from afar and say you'd do it all differently; the truth is, more often than not, we handled everything the best we could with what fight we had in us at the time. It's an unfair judgment we bestow upon ourselves when we weren't meant to comprehend something so twisted and evil.

In my effort to finally get this on paper, I had to relive many moments when I was at my worst. The main thing I gained from that was the realization that I wasn't really crazy…I was learning how to *survive* crazy. Survival isn't always pretty, but it is just that…survival. Surviving is a synonym for *winning* in my book.

Around August of 2013, part of my survival looked like holding onto my estranged friendship with Jamie for reasons that spurred from both a good and bad place. He was a connection to Charlie and a way for me to maintain a positive status quo; in some ways, I guess you could say I used him to maintain my charades from afar.

However, I did enjoy his company, and I did miss our friendship. I chose to forgive him even though he never really apologized to me for his hurtful reaction in hearing what happened with me and Charlie. I still felt afraid to be alone or to lose myself completely with swimming around in my own mind too much. He saved me from both of those fears by giving me something to look forward to and making me laugh.

One night, we were coming back from the movies, and I remember I had been venting to him about everything with Pete and Charlie. I was harsh with my words, and I didn't leave a detail unsaid about what happened after Spring Break, especially regarding my guilt over the fifteen-year-old girl Charlie had been with. I was surprised that Jamie wasn't more disturbed by what happened with that situation…high or not, she was too young to consent to sex considering Charlie was 19 at the time.

My intention in bringing all of that up was to circle back to the night that everything came out publicly. I asked Jamie if he had spoken to Charlie since, and he said that they hadn't talked much at all. And then I asked him to do me a big favor. I wanted to know what Charlie would say about all of it to him if he had no clue that I was listening in. Jamie wasn't thrilled about the idea, but he called him up and put the phone on speaker anyway.

To my dismay, when my name was mentioned, Charlie became upset and blatantly said that *I owed him an apology.* I remember my jaw dropped as I was smoking in Jamie's passenger seat. I couldn't believe the gall he had to say that so bluntly or to frankly even say it at all. I guess deep down, I wasn't surprised by his ugliness anymore, but I wasn't as strong as I thought I was. Hearing him say that definitely cut me and made me regret more than ever that I didn't call things what they were in a much more definitive way when everything first happened.

I don't remember Jamie saying much in response to Charlie or him having any real defense for me at all. This was one of many situations that made it clear to me that I was wrong to have ever thought of Jamie as a "best friend". I knew he wasn't much for confrontation, and he had already shown me that he cared more about himself than he did about me, but it still stung. I was on my own when it came to self-defense. I didn't say a word after that…just absorbed the ugly truth.

I couldn't wrap my brain around how Charlie genuinely acted like he had done nothing wrong to me and, in fact, *acted like I had wronged him! Freaking sociopath* was all I could think in that moment. I was so angry. I remember getting out of the car within minutes of that conversation coming to an end and going to bed. The whole thing was such an unbelievable knife to the heart. *How could I have let this happen to me?* I didn't know how to avenge myself anymore. Every toxic thing I was holding onto to cope with this was continuing to increase my hatred for Charlie and erode away at myself.

The Clinic

I remember feeling so excited when I was selected to work at the clinic. The two girls that worked in my specific department were going to be the ones who had the initial pick out of the five candidates. I heard they even chose me over a pregnant woman.

I really enjoyed my job at first. I worked 10-7 most days, and on Sundays, I worked a morning shift and a late afternoon shift because the clinic closed at 1 P.M..

I ended up connecting with this girl, Amanda, that worked with the technicians. She had already graduated college with a degree in Biology, but she wanted to go back to school to be a licensed vet technician. I was surprised that she was going through that effort because the vets that owned the place were really down to earth people; they would train people up to be technicians themselves. Most of the people on their team had been under them for 5 years or more.

A couple of months into working at the clinic, my Honda had several more issues that were beginning to make it an unreliable vehicle. My dad decided to sell it back to the people we had bought it from and offered to let me trade my grandpa's car in toward one for my 20th birthday. I was grateful for the offer, and I accepted.

Dad and I both have always had a knack for cars, and we

enjoyed searching for prospects together. We ended up finding a pretty good deal on a 2010 Camaro and 2012 370Z. Dad was rooting for the Z, but after test-driving both, I fell in love with the Camaro even though it was a V6. It was also $7k cheaper which sounded way more appealing.

Mom and I took off up North to see my cousins the next day, and I got very well acquainted with my new ride because it was 10 hours each way. Part of my 20th birthday was also this beautiful and very meaningful tattoo that my cousins had designed for me by their tattoo guy. The design captivated me right away; it had my name meaning and my favorite verse beneath it. It was my third tattoo at that point in time and I have no regrets in getting it, or frankly any of the others.

I remember driving to work in my Camaro, and several days passed before anyone noticed it was mine. I never told anyone, but after the girls found out, they started to treat me differently. I began noticing a lot of two-faced interactions and gossip. Then a blunt rudeness ensued with false accusations about various things.

At one point, I was flat-out accused of leaving the water running and flooding our work area when I wasn't even in the building; I was out taking my lunch. I floored it back from Subway, absolutely enraged. For the entirety of my life, I can name numerous occasions that I have been accused of things I did not do. I don't know what it was about me, but it just always felt like I had a sign on my forehead that said please s**t on me, and I was done putting up with it.

I walked into the building with my purse and sandwich in one hand and was holding the phone up to my ear with the other because I was still on the phone with my mom when I bluntly and shamelessly corrected this chick in front of everybody on staff that day. I felt a little bad because I knew it was both girls that accused me, not just her, but since she was the one who sent the text, I felt that the directness towards her made sense at the time.

It turned out the latest girl they hired, who was also extremely rude, had been the one to accidentally leave the water running. She got pulled away to another task and forgot she had plugged the drain. She was an incredibly smart person but super socially awkward and once I realized that she exhibited spectrum-like behavior, I started to not take her rudeness personally.

However, with regards to the other two, I was done.

Apparently, I made the girl who sent me the text cry so badly that she had to leave work…but I did apologize to her when she reached out to do the same over the misunderstanding. Unfortunately, my standing up for myself didn't improve the situation there, and with management aiding and abetting it, I decided to quit not long after that incident as the nonsense continued.

The girls had been taking hour-and-a-half-long lunches and kept me and the other girl waiting every day while they sat in the parking lot, delaying our lunch, amongst other annoying tendencies. If I learned anything from January, it was that trusting in people to do the right thing on your behalf was not a smart move.

My mama always taught me to not worry about other people because they will get what's coming to them; she always encouraged me to stay on my path and fight to stay true to myself. And I did just that by the time I eventually called it quits with this job. I was grateful that a couple of people who noticed the unfairness took it upon themselves to address it when our manager wouldn't. One of the other doctors eventually went out to the girl's truck and forced them to come inside and got on them about the extended lunches.

I was always so grateful for people that would bother to stick up for me because it was such a rarity. Honestly, my mother is the only person who has ever truly come to my defense with the negative things I have experienced in my life. I don't like liars, and I don't tolerate bullies. And once it became clear that this kennel job was a power struggle for these girls, I knew it would have to be short-lived.

The Apartment

During this time, I was beginning to get closer to Josie. I visited her several times, and she came down here on occasional weekends. After a couple of months of getting to know one another more, we decided we wanted to get a place together. She had always wanted to move to the city and get away from her hometown, and I was aching to have a fresh start but not too far from home.

We began making provisions and her dad had offered to cosign for us. We were trying to find her a decent job down here so we could get an idea of our affordability. I ended up getting her a job through a mutual friend when we were closer to our official moving timeline. I had also been seeing this guy I went to high school with named Derek. He and I were never super close in high school, but we always flirted and had a funny relationship.

I knew he had been with many girls, and after my experience with Pete, I certainly didn't want to just hook up with anyone again. Nor was I frankly even wanting to officially date anyone either. I wasn't sure that he understood that, but I didn't try to make it a thing one way or the other because I enjoyed our time together. After a few weeks of hanging out one on one with Derek, I wondered if I was wrong to label him as not being 'boyfriend material.' I wanted to continue getting to know him on the off chance that he was capable of monogamy beneath the surface of everything he put out there.

I introduced him to Josie, and they both smoked weed, so they hit it off. I was not too fond of weed only because it gave me anxiety. The two of them were obsessed with trying to get me to get stoned with them. I don't know what the fascination is for pot heads with trying to get everyone else to partake; perhaps the desire falls into the 'misery loves company category'. I guess it also makes people feel uncomfortable or silently judged when others don't join them in the majority of bad decisions. I ended up joining in on a couple of rare occasions, but I was not a fan.

Through a weird series of events, Josie's dad did not cosign for our apartment. Additionally, in the months leading up to us planning to move in together, my parents were less than pleased with Josie's behavior after she stayed at our house. They were unwilling to cosign because they felt that it was a bad idea. They were right. This conclusion arose after she stayed with us a couple times between January and March.

The first red flags appeared in January. Even though I had to work most days, my parents said Josie was more than welcome to make herself at home whether I was there or not. It was the beginning of January, meaning it had almost been a year since everything had happened with Charlie. I told Josie about what happened with Charlie during one of the weekends I stayed with her a few months before; I disclosed every detail.

I realized that confiding in her about my raw events from the year before was a mistake when January 10th rolled around, and she chose to ditch me for a guy she had just met. The loneliness carried a deeper sting considering the heaviness of that day. When Josie first got to town, we decided to go blow my tax return in the city; we got a hotel room, dressed up, went to a hookah bar, and then walked around afterwards. John had come with us but just wanted to stay back at the hotel and drink.

We were only 20, so we couldn't get in anywhere else but the hookah place. These guys approached us, and it turned out that they were in town for a football game for my hometown team on the West Coast. They were friendly enough, and we had fun walking around with them. We decided to grab some Waffle House before calling it a night. They had Ubered downtown, so they asked us if we could give them a ride back to their hotel. We went into their hotel with them, and after five minutes, they randomly turned the lights out.

Josie was on the bed with her guy, and I was on the pullout couch with the other guy. I was freaking out on the inside the moment it got dark. I didn't know what I was going to do, and I was afraid to leave Josie there if she wanted to stay…thankfully before I could even think about what my next move was going to be, Josie piped up and said my name, "You ready to go?" And I immediately said yes.

The guy found me on Facebook and sent me a baby emoji. I didn't care what some stranger thought of me; I was just grateful I didn't make another huge mistake. After all, I had been through, I already felt stupid enough for letting myself end up in a position like that.

A couple of days later, on the 10th, Josie got picked up by the guy she had been with that night, and she never returned. I was utterly crushed that she would just leave like that, but at the same time, I was also worried about her well-being. My parents were not happy that she left and didn't come back either; it was inconsiderate and concerning.

They began to question my plans to move in with someone who would just go around sleeping with random people like that. They feared what kind of strangers she would bring home to our apartment, and they also already knew she smoked weed because she smelled like it frequently. Weed meant the likelihood of dealers and the type of crowd everyone's parents hope they'll avoid.

They had every right to question all of it and be concerned for me. A year and a half before this, I was about to start college at a beautiful private university, and I had every door open to me. Yet here I was, continuing to spiral in my confusion and hurt as a result of my lack of discernment. I cried myself to sleep, and I kept thinking how much I wished I could go back in time before my life became this empty, lonely mess.

When she was dropped off the next morning, she apologized for leaving. I don't remember what I said in return, but I'm sure I made it okay because I didn't have room for tension with the only friend I had to drink with and confide in. I didn't want to lose that even though she had just shown me how little our friendship really meant to her. The pattern of stupidity and lack of self-respect continued… plus, I had to be at work for a 10-hour shift. We had decided to go shopping at the mall after I got home from work, and I was looking forward to that. I craved having things to keep me going.

Work was becoming a more and more depressing experience as management continued to let the girls act like they were our superiors even though we held the same title. I remember I would routinely just start deep cleaning things because that was our threatened punishment if we refused to be their personal slaves. Rather than wait for the inevitable, I decided to take that power away from them by choosing to deep clean on my own fruition. It was nice because I could be alone and closer to the technicians if they needed assistance. The girls hated that, which made it that much sweeter.

Derek, Josie, and I wanted to find a place to live, and since we didn't have a cosigner, we figured we might as well move in together and not need anyone else's help. In the weeks leading up to this, Josie (while knowing Derek and I sort of had a thing) began making moves on him, and because I had declined to be Derek's girlfriend, he started to treat her the same as me. In all fairness, that was a totally understandable decision on his part. I was afraid of making another mistake, but I still enjoyed his company and thought our friendship was special. I also thought that maybe one day he would prove me wrong... perhaps he wasn't typical; maybe he would fight for me, and then I'd know he was a safe bet. However, the more Josie sought him out, the more flirtatious he was in return. This caused me to step back a bit.

I think what hurt the most about the whole thing was how Josie literally said she would not move in with Derek and me if we continued to go out together, kiss, hug, etc. I held up my end of that agreement. Then, within 48 hours of us living together, I woke up to find them in Derek's bed together. He had proven that my hesitations to be exclusive with him were valid; he was an opportunistic player. But when it came to Josie, I felt like I had been run over by a truck. I knew she slept around semi-frequently, too, but I had confided in her that the only reason I initially declined to be Derek's girlfriend was out of fear of getting hurt. And, of course, I respected her wishes once the move was official so she wouldn't feel uncomfortable living with us. It felt like she stabbed me in the back.

There had been some signs on her part that she was opportunistic as well, but I was still surprised she'd do that to me; I thought we were friends. I didn't listen to my instincts before signing the lease. Nor did I listen to my parents, and boy, did I regret it. I remember the first night we moved in, I got off work, and they had gone to get weed and alcohol and threw a party. I participated and drank a ton before passing out around 3 A.M.. I had to be at work by 7 A.M., so I was beyond hungover. I threw up in the bushes twice while walking the dogs. I barely got through that shift. Josie's job hadn't started yet, so she was at the apartment getting things all set up on her side of our room when I got home from work that night. I had barely moved anything over from my parents' and hadn't even bought myself a bed, so I was still sleeping on the floor.

The next morning, I woke up and Josie wasn't in our room. I remember walking down the hallway towards Derek's bedroom, and to my surprise, I saw her in bed with him. I felt betrayed even though I knew that it wasn't like he was my boyfriend. It was the principle of it, and it just seemed very two-faced of her to ask me to not so much as kiss him, but then she had sex with him at the very first opportunity. Living together put such an additional awkward strain on all of it. I decided that I needed to move out. I had a bad feeling that things would only get worse if I stayed and I didn't want to have even more hurt come from that situation.

I told them that I planned to move out in light of what happened. I said I had no hard feelings towards either of them and hoped we could still be friends, but I explained that this living scenario wasn't for me. I knew surely Josie would get that since she had just said the same thing to me a month prior regarding Derek and I. Josie cried and didn't say much, and Derek walked out, but not before punching the wall. They didn't have another roommate lined up yet, but I told them they could keep my first month's rent, and that would give them four weeks to find someone new. Derek knew a lot of people. This all sounded good and well in my mind; I felt like I was standing up for myself in the nicest way I possibly could in this situation without being ugly back. As hurt as I was, I think I knew deep down they were a much better fit, romantically and friend-wise.

Unfortunately, there was no getting out of this lease. Per my agreement, the office said they would not let me out until April of the following year, even if we found someone to replace me. In other words, I could leave physically, but I'd still be liable financially. I was so angry because I knew Derek and Josie wouldn't fight to find someone to take my place if they knew I was trapped within the contract. If by some miracle they did find someone, having my name attached to theirs also scared me; after the first night of partying, thoughts of structural damage, amongst other things, entered my mind. For all I knew, I'd get lumped in with all kinds of things at this point. All I could think was, why didn't I listen to my parents? I was so ashamed to go home and tell them about this disaster I was stuck in.

My mom and dad had every right to turn their backs on me and tell me good luck with my poor choices, but instead, they loved me through it. This response was actually not very surprising if you were to know them. My mom was lit up over them being in bed together after everything Josie had said to me regarding Derek and I. Mom knew I had been played, and she and Dad both offered to try and help me navigate this with the leasing office.

After some serious thought on all of my options, I decided to just officially move into the apartment and make a third of it my own. My mom was sick to her stomach at the thought of me basically being forced to move back in there and kept begging me to let them try to buy out my contract. I refused. They had been through enough at my expense. I wouldn't let them bail me out of this disastrous move I made that they practically begged me not to do in the first place.

About a week later, I told Derek and Josie that the office refused to let me off the lease for the year even if we did find somebody else. To say it was awkward moving back in was an understatement. They had been 'playing house' from what I could tell, and they were both not really speaking to me. Dad came in and helped me set up my new frame for my day bed. I'm not sure if Derek was home or not, but Josie was. I think she was too ashamed to face my dad because she avoided him the entire time he was there. I could tell it really hurt my dad to leave me there that night; I felt guilty for not being more discerning of the people in my life once again.

I decided to just smile and make the best of it as I dove into unpacking. It was my first time getting one of those mattresses in a box, and it was the most comfortable thing I had ever laid on. I hung up a million pictures and sprayed as much happiness as I could all over my side of the bedroom to cover up how hurt I was feeling about everything.

Twisting the Knife

Josie walked into our room about an hour after I had been hanging things up. I think she was surprised that I was so upbeat and nice despite the depressing predicament she and Derek had put me in. I remember that she tried to blame me for why she had fallen for him. She said that I wasn't around much in the weeks leading up to our moving in, and that when I was around, I had been acting differently. I reminded her that all of the times that I wasn't around, I was at work. I also told her that she really let me down when she ditched me that night in January.

I continued in my honesty and told her that I felt like she treated my parents' house like a hotel, and not long after that week she stayed with us, it began to feel like she wanted to spend more time with Derek than me whenever she visited. I said that if I seemed different back then, it was because her actions had been a bit of a slap in the face, and then, to top it off, this whiplash move she pulled with Derek felt very catty. So now here we were, everything out in the open, and there wasn't much left to say. I think she felt dumb for even trying to put the blame on me after I listed out the bullet points of her choices that caused a natural separation between us.

I finally broke the awkward silence when I asked her if they were in a relationship. Her response spoke volumes about what a terrible friend she was. She said that since I left, it sort of took the 'spark out of things,' and she didn't know what they were or if she had real feelings for him. I started to laugh when she said all of that out loud…did she not realize how horrible that sounded, or was she too high to have a conscience?

When I left, "It took the spark out of things"? So basically, you got pleasure out of hurting me?! *Wow*. Duly noted, I thought. I just chuckled and kept putting my side of the room together. I was extra edgy at work for the next few weeks because of everything I was dealing with at the apartment. I should have been smart enough to know that selfish people that get high night and day aren't capable of loyalty. Loyalty involves self-sacrifice and authenticity.

I knew they didn't grow up with the kind of parents I did, and I always tried to open up my home to them, hoping that we'd all be like family. I did that with practically everyone who ever called themselves my friend. I just couldn't seem to find anyone who truly cared for me the same way in return.

Josie had done some very sweet things for me in the past. I had confided in her, and I had trusted her. And now look, I thought…more of the same, just with different people. I already carried regrets with sharing my past with Josie due to her lacking friendship, but to top it off, she also made me feel bad for talking about it on a venting basis. She said that I needed to 'get over that' and move on. I know I talked about it a few times, but I think after not talking about it for 6 months and dealing with so much negative aftermath as a result, I had to release it as needed.

I drank nearly every night, but Derek and Josie got high around the clock. Derek would go to work high almost daily and even dropped a car on his hand once because he was so stoned. He refused to go to the emergency room out of fear of losing his job at the shop; it never motivated him to stop smoking prior to work though. I also remember Josie running out of weed at one point, and suddenly she was a wreck. She couldn't stop crying and was practically in a panic, having to live without the comfort of the daily fog that intercepted her view on reality.

People who are high 90 percent of the time don't tend to have the capacity to deal with anything real. I knew they were clearly running from stuff, too, but it always hurt that Josie made me feel small for needing to talk about my past when she couldn't even handle her present without being high. After the last several weeks leading up to this, I'm sure, deep down she realized that our friendship wasn't all we had built it up to be; we were too different. I felt that way in January, but I still made the decision to honor our plans. And now here we were, stuck in a very uncomfortable situation for an entire year.

The following two weeks, I was fairly isolated from Derek and Josie. We only saw each other coming and going from work or in the evenings. I would often be at my parents' or return to the apartment to find them leaving to go to TJ's (a friend of Derek's).

I got a bottle of tequila for all of us through TJ because he was of age the first night we moved into the apartment. The two of them apparently drank that same bottle of Tequilla the night that they first slept together. One night, I came home as they were about to leave, and I remember Derek begrudgingly telling me I needed to pay TJ back for it. I didn't even get to drink a drop of that, and he knew it. They both knew the truth, and I didn't care. I didn't want to fight about anything anymore. I was tired of hurting. Tired of being angry. Tired of mess after mess after mess. Especially after learning some horrible rumors from my friend Carmen.

The End of Silence

To give some background, Carmen and I met at the same time as Jessica and me, but we didn't see each other as frequently. She went to State with Charlie, and they occasionally ran into each other. She had met Charlie through me and Jessica when we house-sat and had friends over to hang out with us about three years before this. A few months before moving in with Derek and Josie, I went over to see Carmen and the mutual friend that I asked to help get Josie her job.

We went and grabbed a bite to eat, and afterwards, we came back to Carmen's parents' house to hang out because she was staying there that weekend. It was then that I became aware of how Jessica didn't really care about me either.

Jessica had told Carmen about Charlie and me, but not under the truthful context of what occurred. This came up when Carmen randomly mentioned that she had run into Charlie on campus at Starbucks. She could see the change in my face and said that Jessica told her what happened between us.

I asked to know what Jessica had told her because, as I said before, Jessica never so much as asked me how I was doing with that whole situation, even though she was the first one to hear of it and to call what happened rape. She said Jessica told her that Charlie and I had sex, and he screwed me over. I couldn't believe it. I knew Jessica to have her catty moments, but to say such a blatant lie was so hurtful.

Now, all I can say in her defense is, I tried to deny that it was rape, so maybe in her mind, she didn't see it as a violation after what I said. Maybe from her perspective, it seemed like he had just screwed me over. Regardless, I was still hurt that she would share my personal business on such a sensitive topic with anyone without clearing it with me first. Out of humiliation, I felt the need to clarify and told Carmen what really happened. *Not that the truth was any less humiliating.*

She told me about her encounter with Charlie at Starbucks and said that he asked about me and how I was doing. This was the first I had heard of him kindly asking about me since everything came out publicly with Pete's big mouth. According to Carmen, she told him that I was doing awesome. I was grateful for that because even though that had been highly untrue, I never wanted Charlie to think that he ruined me. I wanted him to believe that I was untainted by him and doing just fine. I asked Carmen if she saw him often. She said they didn't talk much, but she said she would see him playing and singing Christian songs almost daily when she'd be coming to and from the library. *Of Course*, I thought.

Back to the present day at my ever-darkening apartment, I

got a message from Carmen that Charlie hadn't changed a bit. She told me that she had heard rumors that he assaulted one of her sorority sisters in some sort of shower situation. I didn't know the details, and neither did Carmen, but I wanted to throw up. I learned this the same night that Derek was pushing me to pay TJ back; I was so consumed with guilt over this news that I didn't care about something as small as twenty dollars.

I knew I needed to say something. The silence had gone on for too long.

After Derek and Josie left for TJ's that night, I finally had the guts to say something to Charlie through messenger. I called him out on his fake Christian BS and threatened to expose him if I continued to hear of him raping other girls. I also called him out on his unbelievable statement regarding me owing him an apology that I witnessed him saying over the phone that night with Jamie several months before.

I was surprised to find that he responded to my message immediately. I had been drinking, so I was in a somewhat heightened state of emotion and didn't expect what came next. It went from anger and preparation for a war with him to a sudden dismantling of those feelings with his unsuspecting kindness and apologetics.

He denied my accusations and then jumped right into how

he has been under "spiritual attack" because he had been trying to seek God more than ever in his life. He told me that he thought of me daily and, in summary, how he "pained in his heart violently for our friendship because while he didn't think there was rape, he knew if he hadn't pushed me so hard sexually that our friendship wouldn't have been destroyed." He admitted that I asked him to stop multiple times and that he pushed and pushed. He went on to say that he had never known anyone to be as kind or innocent as me and that I always put others first. He said that I was "irreplaceable" and that "we both shared the same scar on our souls."

In that same paragraph, he said that he had feelings for me back when everything happened, and he was afraid to tell me how he really felt at the time. He added that he wanted to apologize to me for all of his wrongdoings, not the other way around. Lastly, he also shared with me that he may have a cancerous tumor in one of his kidneys.

I had no idea where to put all of this. I knew in my heart that I longed for peace in my life, so I ultimately made what I thought was the best decision for me. Since nothing could be undone, I decided the best thing would be to try and have some sort of forgiveness if all seemed genuine. Additionally, I thought that getting a glimpse into his new 'spiritual journey' and 'accountability' he claimed to hold steadfast to would provide some insight for the sake of others.

I felt guilty for caving so quickly, especially if these rumors I'd just heard were true. If I'd had contact with the fifteen-year-old girl and whoever Carmen had told me about through the grape vine, I don't think I would have heard him out at all. But since I didn't, and I wasn't sure of anything, I continued in my weakness and in my desires for all of this to just 'go away'. I still wanted a deeper apology, and I wanted to see that Charlie was on the better path he claimed to be on. I guess I thought experiencing and seeing those things for myself might give me the freedom I'd been so thirsty for.

Once he saw my defenses coming down a little, he wanted to call me immediately. I told him I had been drinking, so that probably wasn't the best idea, but he called anyway, and we spoke briefly. He said that he wanted to see me, hug me and tell me how sorry he was for everything in person. I know this all sounds so stupid, but at the time, I truly thought forgiving him would free me from the hell I was in within my heart. I just wanted to find myself again. I was tired of being lost in this mess. I found a small ounce of hope that forgiveness could be possible if I were to give it a chance and if all the things he said held water. I prayed peace would follow this decision rather than more regret.

A few days later, we made plans for me to come to him because of his kidney situation. He was taking it easy at his place because of the bleeding. He said his roommates were home, so I wasn't worried about us being alone. I remember getting a 20 to bring to TJ's on my way to see Charlie that night. Derek and Josie were already over there hanging out. My nerves were kicking in, and I felt shaky as I geared up for the unknowns of the evening. I asked TJ to meet me outside, and when he retrieved the 20, he told me I didn't need to pay him back. I think he knew that I had been screwed over in the roommate scenario and felt bad for me.

I thanked him and told him to keep it anyway. He invited me to come in, but I told him I had to be somewhere. I pealed out, and I remember listening to Bring Me to Life by Evanescence on repeat until I arrived at Charlie's condo 45 minutes later. I was sitting outside in my car for a minute, contemplating whether or not I was making a mistake in doing this. I knew that this was crazy in more ways than one. But everything that happened to me was *crazy*. I had to cope with crazy either way, so I figured I might as well try to find some way to live with this, even if it looked ridiculous.

After all, partying and numbing myself wasn't working, and being angry had only hurt me more. I saw the front door open, and he stood within the frame, smiling at me. I opened my car door and smiled back as I approached him. He reached out for a hug; he had warned me that he planned to hug me for a very long time. And he did.

Flicker of Hope

When I went inside, I sat on the couch and began to catch up on life with Charlie. He told me all about his medical stuff and the unknowns he was faced with potentially having a cancerous tumor in his kidney. Then he told me about some songs he had been writing; he played a clip of one he wrote about me and our broken friendship.

The lyrics confused me in that they referred to him having to carry all of the blame for losing our friendship. It *was* entirely his fault. I didn't say anything, just took the words in. I knew in his mind he didn't rape me, but what he admitted to doing via messenger *was rape*, even if he didn't understand that.

How could I find peace in this if he wasn't even going to fully admit and apologize for what he had done? What was I thinking? The song lyrics brought my naïve stupidity to the surface, and I felt a small pit in my stomach forming. But I was here already...I was in this. Maybe he would own all of it in time instead of just parts of it? Maybe I'd still find healing somehow if we could talk about everything on a deeper level?

After I got home that night, I had mixed feelings, but I remember being grateful to have put the anger behind me in some form. That was enough for me at the time, especially in my situation with the apartment. I felt released from some of this, just enough to have a spring in my step filled with hope that I was in control again…and that I could write a happier ending to my story.

I remember Charlie texting me that he felt tremendous joy after I left that night, knowing that our friendship wasn't dead. I was still getting used to the idea of him experiencing any happiness at my expense again. But the vulnerability was explorative and successful as it freed a part of me that seemed forever bound in anger. I told him that I had found relief in this too because at the time, that was the truth. It wasn't everything I'd hoped it would be, but it felt like a start in a positive direction.

Work seemed to feel lighter. The apartment mess felt surprisingly livable. And I began to feel untouchable from all those who seemed to want to cause me pain because the thing that had been hurting me the most had subsided to a better place. Josie began to come around, and it was clear that whatever had happened between her and Derek had faded. Whether that was because of me no longer being hurt in the process or not, I didn't care anymore. I was free of that too.

As I said before, I felt like they were a much more suitable match, and I found relief that I could set my stakes higher. I had gone out to lunch with my mom and told her everything that happened with Charlie. I was so afraid of her judgement, but I was again met with understanding. She wasn't happy that I had Charlie back in my life, but she was grateful that I was seemingly more myself than I had been in over a year. She found relief in that and respected my right to use the most illogical approach to accomplish it. I think her reaction was partly because she was afraid to lose me; until this untimely breakthrough, I had been so lost in all of it.

In that same conversation, she tried to convince me to quit my job and return to school full-time. I had talked about applying to State because they had a better list of programs for Criminal Justice, which had begun to capture my interest. I had been an undecided major when I was still attending Westwood. I had thoughts extending all over the map on various career paths.

I think the main reason I never could settle on anything was because my whole life, I'd always wanted to get married young, have kids young, and be a stay-at-home mom. I never truly sought out a career. I knew I loved helping people and animals through various volunteer jobs I had in the past, but I wasn't sure what would make the most sense for me to settle on with my studies. Looking back, writing would have been a fairly obvious choice for me to focus my attention. However, my experiences turned my head towards sex trafficking and seeking justice for those who have lived in suffering. My story pales in comparison, but even the small taste I had in feeling like my body was not my own pushed my desires to help those who have undergone a true living hell.

I agreed to apply to State and decided that I would quit my job at the next opportunity that seemed fitting between now and the end of the summer. Things had not improved whatsoever in that department and the thought of being able to be done with that drama did give me some satisfaction. Sure enough, an opportunity arose when the girls pegged our manager to host another meeting regarding our lack of "respect" for them; we were clueless about what else we could do to meet their odd expectations. I came to work to work, not to kiss anyone's a**. And I worked my a** off every day and frankly exceeded my requirements. These additional hoops were laughable and something I decided I wouldn't tolerate.

Upon hearing about this upcoming meeting, I suspected this was another "power trip" discussion. I told the new girl that if this meeting was about what I thought it was about, I would be putting in my notice just out of the shear need to be done with the condescension and stupidity.

It turned out I was exactly right, and to their dismay, they got their wish before the meeting was finished, just not in the way they wanted it. They wanted to be in control of everything, be the boss, and make us feel beneath them…well perfect, I decided to let them have the whole department to themselves and the shifts they hated. I smiled so brightly that I lit up the room every day for the remaining two weeks that I was there.

I had mixed feelings about my parents paying my rent for the remainder of my lease, but after learning that it was significantly cheaper than campus living, I felt some relief. I got my acceptance letter a few weeks later and was gearing up for classes to start. Derek and Josie were very judgmental and treated me as if I were completely spoiled for choosing to quit my job and go back to school full-time. This decision did not impact them, and I resented that they acted like it was any of their business.

Two years' prior, Derek had received a full track scholarship and had blown it off after only a year. And Josie went to community college and dropped out after only one semester. I decided that I wouldn't be made to feel selfish or spoiled for taking an opportunity I was given simply because they chose to squander theirs. My grandfather had always wanted to pay my way through college, so I was certainly blessed, but again, I felt it was unfair for them to hold that against me. Especially after all I had always tried to share with them when it came to my family.

Charlie and I had stayed in touch and exchanged texts mostly. There wasn't anything deep said between us, but the texts weren't very humorous either; I preferred it that way. I was highly sensitive to what Charlie considered 'funny' because of his past treatment of me, so I was glad he just stuck to keeping things friendly. I wouldn't have been able to handle him acting like we could just pick up where we left off or like nothing bad had ever happened.

What we had left still needed a lot of rebuilding for healing to take place for me in the long run, and no matter what, I knew it would always be different. Taking things slow was working for me, and having him back in my life as a distant 'friend' was continuing to bring me relief from the past, as odd as it sounds.

I remember him still going through a lot with his kidney situation, but I don't know if he had done the biopsy to find out if it was cancerous at that point yet or not.

I got a text from him one night that he would be playing guitar downtown and he invited me to meet up with him if I was free. It was a semi-chilly night, and I remember feeling nervous but also somewhat excited to see him. We hadn't seen each other in person since our talk at his place.

Forgiveness felt good. Letting go of all of this darkness felt incredible. And being able to be happy in spite of my crappy living situation felt invigorating.

Cold Water

He was still singing when I got there. After the last song, he packed up his guitar and walked to my car with me. There was something in the air that night that reminded me of the old us…*laughter and adventure*. He wanted to take a drive with me, and we went on back roads that we had never been on together.

After blowing through nearly a quarter tank of gas, we were sitting at a red light, and he randomly said, "Let's drive to Alabama!" I started laughing and questioned why Alabama. He said that one of his dad's shops was down there, and we could hang out. I laughed once more but shot that idea down.

However, I felt like a movie might be nice, so I asked if he would want to come by my apartment. I hadn't told him the details of what went on with Derek and Josie, but he knew that I was living with them.

Josie was out of town that weekend, and Derek had just turned 21, so I wasn't sure if he'd have company or be out with friends. Charlie said that was good with him, even with the unknowns of who would be there, so we went. When we got there, Derek wasn't home. I showed him my picture wall behind my bed, and he noticed I kept up one picture of a bunch of us from high school at one of his bonfires. I think he was surprised to see that I had kept that memory up where I could see it every day. We went out to the living room couch, and I showed him some stuff that I had written. He knew that I was into writing and seemed to think the stuff I showed him was good. After a few minutes, we started a movie. He was on one part of the couch, and I was on the other when it began.

After about 20 minutes or less, he had moved closer and started cuddling me. Some part of me was hoping he would, if I'm honest. I really can't answer why that is, not even now, but there was something within my heart that still cared for him. His touch made me feel the same feelings as before…rather than repulsion, I somehow felt some form of comfort.

How? How could I find any comfort cuddling with the guy that broke my heart and raped me simultaneously? I was miles away from sanity as the night continued. At first, everything felt as though it were in slow motion. Him slowly moving beside me, our arms touching, followed by our hands, and eventually our lips. Before we kissed, I remember Derek coming home.

He knew what had happened with Charlie because I told him things when we were sort of 'seeing each other' before all the Josie drama. I was surprised he didn't say anything when he came in; I figured he'd take the opportunity to call me out for my stupidity. He got something out of his room and left within a minute of coming home. I didn't think he would return for hours, but oddly, returned almost 30 minutes later. That was not like him at all. He'd been staying out until 1 or 2 in the morning ever since he had turned 21.

He later shared with me that it was out of concern for me that he didn't stay out longer. I appreciated that. I'm sure he felt like I was a nut case…after all, I was living out the definition of insanity…*again*. He had known Charlie in high school, too. In fact, he was in the same picture that I showed Charlie when we first got to the apartment. Sadly, we were all far beyond our simple and blissful bonfire night memories. Derek didn't know that I had tried to make peace with Charlie because I still felt like I was in a war zone with him after the Josie situation. Not that I would have necessarily told him about any of my personal stuff anyway at that point.

He had continued to ice me out even though whatever "romantic" situation between him and Josie had ceased to exist. Maybe he blamed me for that, too? I had no clue. And I could have cared less at that point in time. I had been friendly even in the midst of being screwed over by both of them, so I figured if he wanted to judge me, I had every right to go off on him. This was none of his business and thankfully, he never tried to make it his business either.

The movie began to fade away as Charlie and I started making out. I remember things got intense fairly quickly and it was almost as if we picked up right where we left off the last time we were in his truck. That scared me a little as I feared how this would end. I couldn't understand why I felt so captivated by him…how could I want him to hold me this close and touch me this way? Some anxiety emerged at the unknowns and at the realization that we could never be anything real after all he had done.

My family would never accept him, and why should they? Why should I? *What was I doing?!* These thoughts trickled into my head, but the pleasure of the moment overthrew my sense of logic. Now things were complicated again, I thought to myself. How am I going to navigate *this*?

The most twisted thing about it all was his kiss and how it made me feel. I felt this sense of *relief*…a passion ensued that I had never felt before, not even with my first love. I felt so intimately connected to this guy. The guy who had ripped me apart just a little over a year before. I couldn't stop longing for each touch, each kiss, and each exhilarating feeling I was having in this moment with him.

I was drifting into a coma as we lay there on the couch, enthralled with one another, when suddenly, I felt his teeth sink into my skin…hard! *Yes, he pulled a move from Ted Bundy's playbook*…he had done this once before after we had been wrestling around and it was extremely odd to me then. It was even more strange to me now because this time, it happened when we were being intimate with one another.

Was that enough to wake me up? No. I shoved his head away out of instinct and said *ouch,* abruptly. However, he kept trying a few more times to bite my arm, my leg, and even my shoulder. It was a mood killer for sure and I just remember asking him what he was doing. He grinned and persisted a few more times. I was highly inexperienced, but even in my lack of expertise with foreplay, I didn't feel that the biting of random body parts belonged in the pool of pleasurable fixations. At least not for me.

After he realized that was beginning to turn me off, he stopped and went back to trying to hold me close and making out with me. Truthfully, that was all I had wanted. I wanted to be held by him. The kissing felt right even though I knew deep down it was wrong. I can't explain it, but I guess when it was slow and deep, it didn't feel like he was just kissing my lips…it felt like he was kissing my scars. And that felt like a remedy…a replacement for all the pain.

I hadn't wavered from my past desires to find peace in this, but I never knew what could bring *lasting* peace to such a distorted mess. I guess the sad conclusion I found in that moment was simple… *I wanted him to love me so I could stop hating myself.* It's hard to admit that, but it was the truth. As unfathomable as that was, I just hoped I could find healing in our own little bubble. And the thought of feeling more whole with him made me bulletproof when it came to the potential judgment of others. I was mentally preparing my heart that this might be a thing we do. I might have a new secret, but one that's not eating me alive this time.

Wrong.

In what world would having a secret relationship with your ex-best friend/rapist be something that brings you healing?? I swear I just wish I could go back in time and smack myself in the face.

He took my hand and guided me from the couch to my bedroom. It reminded me of the first night we kissed at my parents' place. I was beginning to feel nervous about his expectations and how that had gone before. I felt that after all the grace I had chosen to extend, he would surely respect me, and thankfully that was proven true. However, there were some revolving PTSD moments wrapped up in this night because he tried very hard to get me to change my mind. *Over and over and over.*

He offered to go down on me or do any position I wanted. I told him I was afraid for us to cross that line, and I didn't want to ruin this. *Something I hoped he valued as much as I did.* I was still making out with him, and in our passion and stupidity, we had both gotten down to our underwear. Come to think of it, I'm pretty sure his were now on the floor, but I kept mine on. At that point, I was beginning to clench up the more he kept asking me to reconsider sex. I came up with a secondary excuse about our lack of protection.

He piped up immediately, saying, "Plan B." Plan B…as in

the pill I took the following night after the rape. *That was it…that was the kicker* that woke me up enough to stop dancing that grey line with him. The fact that he brought that up so casually was proof that he clearly did not understand the magnitude of hurt he caused me before.

In my idiotic attempts to hold onto the "good" from the night, I shoved the Plan B comment down into the ugly trenches of the past. I just wanted to snuggle up to him and sleep and pretend that somehow everything would be okay. I didn't want to return to everything being so bleak and awful again, even though I was already combating red flags.

Unfortunately, after the passion and heat of the moment were gone, reality set in much faster than I was prepared for. He said that cuddling wasn't his thing a couple of minutes after I awkwardly tried to lay my head on his chest. He sat up and started to talk about needing a ride back to his truck. In the short span of time in my room, as we got dressed, I learned several things that immediately ruined my hope for this redemption to last between us.

I was afraid to have him act weird after being intimate with me, and I wanted to know what this meant to him and for us from now on. I felt sick because the last time I asked him that question was prior to the rape, and he crushed me by saying it was just a "lust thing."

I tried to broach the topic with kid gloves because I didn't want him to assume I was trying to make us a label or anything either; I just wanted to know how we'd navigate our friendship in light of this. It felt like someone threw a cold bucket of water at my face when I took in what he said next…he said he really shouldn't have done any of that with me because he was in a relationship!!! Not just any relationship, a relationship with a 17-year-old girl he said he had planned to marry...some sweet, innocent, Christian girl who had been homeschooled her whole life. I remember he showed me her picture.

I sat there in disbelief but was afraid to let any of my vulnerability show, so I tried to hide it by rushing us out the door. I told him that I agreed that we shouldn't have done any of that and put my stealth face on. I was disturbed. I was raw. I was angry. I was humiliated. I was hurt. I was confused. I was *all the things apart from <u>awake</u>*. Even over a year later, I found myself in the same repetitive cycle of being so deeply lost and doing the craziest things in hopes of being released from the grips of the past.

You stupid girl. How could you let him that close? Close enough to where he could actually hurt you again! *You idiot.* As if this twisted forgiveness concept wasn't enough, you leave him a perfect runway to do more damage? The voices in my head were livelier than I cared for them to be at 5 A.M., but they were right. All of this had been a terrible idea from the beginning.

The 30 minute drive to his truck was killer. I had a cigarette in my center console, and I could hardly wait to light it up after dropping him off. I was very selective with the songs I played on the ride back. I recall playing Better Days by The Goo Goo Dolls and Far From Home by Five Finger Death Punch. Both songs somehow encapsulated the mixed emotions I was juggling after such an abrupt thrust into the reality of my false hope. He showed interest in the songs and seemed to take in the lyrics. He also appeared to tune in to the change in my disposition; I don't think he knew what to do.

He didn't say much else to me on the ride home, not even with the usual nervous energy he always had. The early morning hour and lack of sleep could have accounted for the silence, but I still assumed guilt had something to do with it. I just tried to maintain some semblance of dignity in the ashes of whatever 'this' was.

As we approached his truck, I didn't say much in our goodbye. Driving home, I felt so empty. I didn't know what to make of everything and I figured dissecting it would only make me feel worse. Clearly, he didn't care about me or my healing at all. He wasn't sorry for anything he'd ever done based on his actions. It felt like he severed my scar tissue and dumped a heaping scoop of salt all in it. I didn't think I would be hearing from him anytime soon, considering the news of his girlfriend and the fact that, once again, he knew I was not going to let him have sex with me. Apparently, that was all he still desired.

He said that he had a good relationship with the girlfriend's parents. A part of me quivered at the thought of him being with her physically; she looked like she was twelve. Was he calculated, or was he just opportunistic? It felt like the night we spent together was opportunistic, but what if I was wrong? What if he was some calculated monster? I felt like everything I ever said regarding him using his music and his 'Christian front' like a wolf in sheep's clothing was probably always accurate. I had fallen for it, too, and I, of all people, shouldn't have been so easily fooled. Especially not after everything that happened the year before.

Free Falling

I was surprised that a few hours later, he called me, but it wasn't to talk about anything regarding us; he left his guitar in the trunk of my car. Josie had just arrived back at the apartment when he and I had made plans to meet up later for him to retrieve it. I wanted to tell her everything…a few months before, I would have, but I didn't trust her now. I didn't want her to know how much of an idiot I had just been, or how I was falling apart on the inside over all of it. For all I knew, she'd take pleasure in my pain as she had before.

I was happy Charlie and I would have another chance to talk, but not because I wanted to see him again. I just wanted to ensure that I left things on my terms, and I felt like the way the night unfolded didn't leave me in the best position. I needed to reflect nothing but confidence in order to hold my head high. I felt like he had pulled one on me, like he was just seeing how far he could take this before doing whatever best suited him. I decided it was time to put up my walls again, but I would be smarter this time. *Clearly, I learned nothing from the year before.*

Carmen, Jessica, and our other mutual friend Zoe had invited me out to grab lunch. I told Charlie that I could meet up with him after that. I remember I had a spring in my step and a smile on my face despite feeling like I was in another world of hurt and unknowns. My "fake it till I make it" mantra kicked in and I began to regroup. I knew that I had another shot at pretending I was fine, and I wasn't going to mess it up.

Being vulnerable or real with him was no longer an option, so I needed to find a discrete way to keep the ball in my court while staying as detached as possible. I didn't want to go back to being enemies, but I knew I couldn't allow him to be too close to me either. Things had to be somewhere in between for me to maintain some control in this pitiful scenario.

When I arrived at Sonic to meet him, the exchange was quicker than I expected, but I rolled with it. He was being jokey with me and acting like nothing had happened between us. As the cuts felt deeper than ever, I managed to keep smiling through the pain. I reciprocated however he was towards me to salvage my armor from anymore heavy artillery repercussions. As far as he was concerned, I was as happy as I appeared to be.

The next day, Jessica asked me if I'd go with her on a Tinder date to ensure the guy wasn't a creep. I agreed despite the recent betrayal I felt after learning that she shared my personal business with Carmen. I didn't have room in my heart to hold onto anything else during that time.

We decided to reach out to Ralph because the guy she was meeting lived on the same side of town as him. We stopped by and hung out with him and his friends before going on this "date." Jessica didn't tell me they planned to meet at the dude's house until we were halfway there. All the more reason that I didn't want her to go alone. Charlie had been texting me off and on since he picked up his guitar from me the day before.

All I could do was think about how, a little over 24 hours earlier, we were wrapped up in each other before he dropped two bombs on me. I couldn't stand to be in my skin the more I thought on all of it. I was so grateful to have the distraction with Jessica and it was nice to see Ralph. It was the first time since our breakup that we'd seen one another outside of when I returned some of the old T-shirts he had lent me. That made me ache on the inside because I would have given anything to go back in time and do it all differently.

When we arrived at the Tinder dude's house, it was obvious that he and Jessica weren't hitting it off. We sat in the garage with the door open. Shortly after, the guy had a friend that pulled into the driveway. He had just come back from a wedding and was clearly intoxicated.

He was quite cocky, and frankly, had he not been funny, I wouldn't have found him attractive. He was tall, not the skinniest, but not fat either. We sort of had to carry the conversation because Jessica and her guy kept running out of things to talk about. We mostly just began picking at each other in a series of sarcastic banter.

A little while later, the guys were trying to find a way to get into the guest house. I forget why they were meeting us at this house; it must have been a mutual friend's place or a halfway point, but they couldn't access anything but the garage.

The guy I had been flirting with was desperately trying to find a way in so we could get more intimate with one another. I found relief that he couldn't open the door, but that didn't stop me from making out with him. Making out was typically as far as my comfort level would allow.

Once he realized he'd have to break the door to get in, he gave up and approached me. He picked me up and had me up against the outside wall of the garage; I wrapped my legs around him, and we went back to kissing as if we weren't total strangers. It felt like some sexy make-out scene straight out of a movie.

Jessica broke up our little moment together a few minutes later because she was ready to go. The rush of the night's events was just enough to take my mind elsewhere; I found tremendous relief in my escape from all the thoughts plaguing my heart.

Cruel Summer

In the following days, I tried to find the best way to navigate everything with Charlie. The texts he'd send made me feel like I was still in control at first but unfortunately, the conversations were always so fleeting and often left me more depressed. He'd have days where he'd act like he sincerely cared and other days where he was casual and short. Both types of interactions made me feel like I was walking a tightrope with my dignity and emotions. I was so ashamed to feel anything resembling comfort when he'd reach out to me. I didn't want to be dependent on him in any way.

Who clings to their rapist for comfort and control...especially after what he just pulled!? I continued to feel like the most damaged person.

Deep down, I still longed for peace but now more than ever, I felt as though peace would always remain out of reach for me. I was my own worst enemy by keeping Charlie in my life for the same screwed-up reasons I had the year before. This negative cycle of stupidity was taking a toll on my ability to see that I still had such a bright future ahead of me if I'd only let go of this mess.

Meanwhile, nothing had come up about Charlie's girlfriend in our limited text exchanges. I had every right to call him out, but I was too afraid for him to misinterpret my anger for something it wasn't. He'd send me songs he had written or been working on sometimes when he was a little more personal with me. But mostly he'd just send me odd jokes that made little to no sense. I'd reply with the same small talk and random banter, but eventually, it became harder for me to keep up the charades because I just wasn't good at being fake. It became especially difficult for me when he began to dissipate from my life just as quickly as he had reentered it.

I'd grown more depressed and anxious as summer went on because I felt like such a fool for allowing him to hurt me again. Then you add on how he would just leave me in the wings of our little talks, wondering when he'd pop up next…it was just the cherry on top of the s**t Sunday I'd made for myself in all of this. He'd initiate a light-hearted text conversation and then disappear for a week or two, or sometimes even more. I began to reply less and less, and when I would reply, I kept things very curt and to the point. If I couldn't feel in control of the situation, I felt like I was unraveling internally.

I knew I needed to let him fade away. It was causing more damage to allow him to feel the freedom to talk to me whenever he wanted to; I had always intended for this to stay on my terms. I felt like I epically failed, and I just prayed he couldn't see the shambles I was in because of it. It was confusing to navigate because his messages were usually so friendly and upbeat. It made me miss the past. I still couldn't escape my longing for the fall of 2012, especially when I had to look at the bed I'd made for myself in the apartment situation.

I remember this one text exchange we had that was about a month after our most recent physical encounter…I briefly strayed from my walls and shared some of my sadness about all of it. I relayed to him that I missed the old us and wished things didn't have to be so tainted. He replied with the same and added that he felt like we were doing better. That was always the thing that stung the most…the use of the word *we*. I never bothered to separate myself from the word "we" in those conversations we had that year, but it always made me feel like I was owning something that wasn't mine to own. *We* weren't the problem. I *became* my own problem in trying to learn to cope with every ugly thing *he* brought into my life.

At one point, he didn't text me for a whole month that summer, and I felt like I was free falling into unknown territory. I had allowed him back into my life after forgiving the unforgivable. I had allowed him to touch me. I had made everything 'okay' again as far as he was concerned after how he blindsided me in May at my apartment with more lustful intentions and omissions. *How could he just disappear? And more importantly, how much more pathetic could I get?* I wondered both of these things daily as they ate away at my ability to keep up my smile.

The voice in my head that loved to rub my nose in my messes

was constantly having a ball with this one…*You want your rapist to miss you…to fight for you? Seriously? That's a laugh. You deserve to be right where you are, you psycho.* And that's usually the part where I would reach for the next drink every night.

I think that Charlie started to notice that I wasn't okay. I hadn't joked back with him in our last couple of conversations via text. During a big fight at the apartment, I randomly reached out to see if he was home. He replied that he was out of town the next morning and offered to call me when he got off work. I didn't reply. Two days later, I woke up to seven long text messages from him. These were some of the most vulnerable messages I'd ever received from Charlie, and his words genuinely touched me. It made me feel less crazy to see that deep down, some part of him did care.

He said he really didn't want to lose us again. He talked about my heart and said he'd never known someone so innocent and loving as me. He said that I was a challenge and one of his greatest blessings. He wanted to keep pursuing our friendship from a safe distance while he was out of town so that we could rebuild our foundation without being "tempted" to get intimate.

He made it clear that he felt that we could find healing and redemption together. In the apparent struggle to get all of this out to me in writing, he admitted that he was trying to convey how much he missed me and was trying to find the right words to show me how much he loved me and wanted his friend back. He even said he could see us old and grey sitting on a porch one day, feeling grateful we overcame our trials. I longed for every word he said to be true and for him to be capable of rebuilding something with me.

Frankly, I longed for him to carry our friendship for a while so that I could still find healing in it. However, I knew that some things needed to be said.

While I shared some kind remarks about all he said regarding my heart and how I missed our friendship, I finally had the guts to call him out on the last night we were together in May. I owned that I participated in the making out but stated that the other hurtful aspects of that night were entirely on him. For us to be intimate in *any way* with our history was already a lot, but then for him to so casually suggest that we use "Plan B" as a form of contraception was unbelievable.

I told him I felt like he clearly didn't understand what he had done in the past based on how he treated that situation. And, of course, I brought up the fact that he had a *girlfriend* on top of everything else while he was practically naked in bed with me! In my book, it already felt like he used me even though we didn't have sex. I told him that while I missed our friendship too, I felt like a friendship would be impossible for us with how messed up everything was between us. There was too much damage done to ever have anything normal or real.

He first replied, stating, "I know how you feel. You and I share first-hand experience on both sides of that situation." He then disputed that we were not too far gone for a fresh start and continued saying that he believed we could lay a solid foundation from this safe distance. He said he would be gone for a few weeks, giving us time to rebuild. He added that "falling is part of learning how to walk." I didn't know what to make of the first response he sent…it almost felt like he was trying to act like we both went through the same hardships in the past. I was also frustrated that he didn't acknowledge anything I said about having a girlfriend or apologize for anything. However, as usual, I just went with the little peace I could grasp from the kind words he shared in his other texts.

Moments after I "went with it," we returned to having a casual conversation and once again, I didn't truly hold him accountable. In reality, there wasn't anything to rebuild here except for within myself.

This isolated sneak-peak at his affection for me was like a shot in the arm for a few weeks, but like everything else, it wasn't lasting, nor could it compete with the lack of maturity our conversations carried. I needed something real to hold onto and he just couldn't give me that. Even though no real ownership took place on his part, I was relieved that at least I finally said *something* about May.

Bruises

In the following weeks, I continued seeking relief in all the wrong places to no avail. I slipped into an even darker pit with alcohol and bad choices. Bridges were seemingly mended enough with Derek and Josie to where I could socialize with them without the awkward tension.

However, the two of them weren't getting along very well from what I could tell. They would individually include me in whatever they were doing, which mostly involved drinking and smoking weed. I welcomed the chance to get high after the whiplash of events that had been stacking up all summer.

Charlie and I weren't talking as frequently anymore. When we did, he continued to act super casual, hyper, and short with me which stung on levels that exceeded what I imagined after feeling a small semblance of hope again. It wasn't that he was being ugly, but his lack of tenderness towards such a fragile situation is what did me in.

Every time I drank, I felt as though I were trying to numb my sadness over the loss of the temporary peace I had with that whole mess. Allowing him to pop in and out of my life so casually continued screwing with my head just as it always had before. I didn't need one more reason to hate myself, and I regretted ever embarking on a path of forgiveness with him most days.

Derek and I started to grow closer again, and he decided to throw a party with a smaller crowd one night. We had been drinking, and at one point, I remember us joking around about who was tougher than the other. I told him I could take him and stuff like that in what I thought was "good humor."

I guess we were talking about taking punches and who had the most stamina…I'm not entirely sure because I was wasted. Long story short, he ended up knocking me out when he randomly punched me in the face amidst our joking about who was stronger. Obviously, he was…he was 6'3, and I had genuinely been messing around when I said that. I never dreamed he would actually hit me. I blacked out for a couple of minutes, and when I came to, he was in a panic, trying to wake Josie up in her room, saying, "I didn't mean to, I didn't mean to."

One of Derek's friends was trying to tend to me and make sure I was okay. I couldn't feel anything. Then, I saw the video of what happened. (Yeah, someone recorded it.) I saw him hit me so hard that I flew back onto the couch. I ran into the bathroom, saw my puffy lip and jaw, and immediately freaked out.

I was practically in a drunken stupor as I ran out of the apartment in a panic; I just remember trying to hide behind some of the cars in the parking lot. I'm not sure why, honestly. I knew Derek wasn't going to do that again. It was clear that he felt terrible, but I think I just couldn't wrap my pickled brain around why he did it in the first place. Sober now and thinking back on that night, I still don't know what prompted him to do what he did. He had even randomly kissed me earlier in the evening when he taught me how to drive his stick shift in the parking lot. I knew he was clearly drunk when he hit me, but that's still no excuse to do that to someone.

He ran after me and found me hiding beside someone's car. He scooped me up and carried me into his room. Josie had been behind him until he shut his door. I heard her saying my name in the background. I think she knew I was out of my mind between the boos and the blow to my face. I just remember crying and Derek rocking me to sleep in his bed. A few hours later, I vaguely recall stumbling back to my room with a throbbing headache when it was still dark outside.

The next morning, I went into the bathroom and looked in the mirror at the gnarly bruise on my face, all purple and blue. My lip was swollen, and so was my cheek and lower jaw. Derek had gone to work, but Josie was still there. She told me that I should call the police to make a report. I said that wouldn't do me any good. Drinking underage and having another incident where someone hurt me on the record…all I could think was, how much more stupid could I get? I lay in bed for the rest of the day because I was too ashamed to go anywhere.

When Derek came home, I was still lying in bed. He came into my room, sat next to me, and tilted my head to look at what he had done. He laughed and said he couldn't believe I dared him to hit me like that. He said he was sorry as casually as he would have ordered a drive-through meal for lunch. I went out into the living room about twenty minutes later to see him sitting on the couch, sipping a bottle of vodka.

I sat next to him and stared at him for a second. He wouldn't look at me at first. When he finally did, I told him that this changed things between us. I said, even in joking, there's never a time when it's okay to hit a girl. I kept what I said short, and he grabbed my hand and told me he loved me and that he was sorry. This time, he sounded more sincere. I don't remember what I said, but I squeezed his hand before leaving.

I knew I had to face my parents sometime, so I needed to get my story straight. "Slipped in the shower" it was…and I practiced saying it repeatedly to make it believable. My mom could always see right through me, so I needed to get this right. The next day was my orientation at State. Perfect, I thought…so much for a fresh start with this freshly bruised-up face. I was mortified. I felt like my scars were as transparent as my idiocy.

One night, right before school officially began, one of Derek's friends came over to the apartment. I had heard of her the year before through Pete because they used to hang out. I didn't know if she hated me because of all that had gone down with him, but thankfully, he never even came up in conversation. However, what did get mentioned was *much worse*. She sat in front of me on our living room floor and randomly asked me if I was the girl Charlie had "supposedly raped." I sat there in shock, not just at what she asked, but that she felt the freedom to be so bold and candid in my space. Derek and Josie were in earshot of us. I bluntly replied with a question regarding where she heard that from. I figured it was probably Pete, but I wanted to be sure.

To my surprise, she told me that she had heard Jamie talking about it recently. I was livid. Within five minutes of that news, I got on the phone with Jamie and cut him out of my life. That lasted for about a year. He was shocked and hurt, but I didn't care. I was so angry that he'd even begin to talk about my past as if it were his own.

Had he not been so selfish and strange when he first learned about what happened with Charlie the year before, I may have believed him when he tried to deny it. For all I knew, this girl was out to hurt me with her connection to Pete, but regardless, I just needed space from Jamie. My decision felt valid in light of how he acted in the past about everything.

The Dot

After the ups and downs with Charlie, being hit in the face, being betrayed by Jamie, and feeling like my whole world was in shambles, I decided to formally declare to Charlie that I didn't want him in my life anymore either. I told him via text that while I was glad for our "forgiveness," this friendship wasn't healthy for me. He had already slowly begun to disappear from my life, so at least now, this would be on my terms.

I was tired of this scar haunting me at every turn. Regardless of Charlie's take on the past, this scar was mine alone as he was the one who inflicted it to begin with. I resented him trying to act like we both had endured the same pain. I figured that there just wouldn't ever be any real peace for me in this mess. I felt like I had tried everything, and the truth was, all that remained of me was this drunken idiot who kept making poor choices in an effort to seem "fine." It wasn't working...*I wasn't fine* at all. And I was going deeper and deeper into the trenches. Something had to give.

Charlie responded immediately and tried to understand where this was coming from. I told him the truth. I explained how I had just been bombarded with more people bringing up our past. While it wasn't his fault that Jamie was blabbing, it was still a reminder of the ugly parts of our past that still regrettably held me hostage. I mentioned details of the rape that still haunted me, and I referenced May again too.

I told him it was a mistake to act like things could ever be made right with us. The weight of the truth in his actions was too much for my conscience to take. I couldn't pretend anymore, and I said if he ever cared about me at all, he'd let this "friendship" return to being nonexistent. In my heart, I felt like I just needed something from him that I knew he couldn't provide. Some kind of love that, in my messed-up head, would make all of this livable. Not a relationship kind of love, just something more along the lines of caring and protective. *Clearly, that was a ridiculous fantasy that would never come true.* He was not the answer to my problems, he only made more of them.

He sent me a couple of long messages trying to convince me that he really did care about me and that it was his mistake to let things go that far that night at my apartment. He said he didn't mean to be dishonest with me and said that he didn't intend to hurt me. Then, he sent me a picture of a dot and asked me what I saw. I replied simply, "a dot." He tried to equate our issues to that one small dot.

He said everything else around the dot was all the goodness we had shared in our past friendship and could continue to share together now if I'd allow it. He referenced several memories from before the rape that tugged at my heartstrings a bit, but I still didn't budge immediately. I took the time to explain to him how that dot f**ked my whole world up, and it was a much bigger deal than he seemed capable of understanding.

I said that the nights we once shared were beautiful and they'd always be ours; forgiveness (only for the sake of me moving forward) could still exist between us, but I needed him to respect my need for space. I needed to be able to move on, and I couldn't do that with him popping in and out of my life as he pleased.

He called me.

I told him what had happened at the apartment and how I was genuinely unraveling and couldn't handle much else, especially with him. He lost it and acted all protective of me when I told him about getting hit in the face. I found it almost comical to hear him, of all people, acting protective when he had caused the most damage even though, deep down, I longed for him to care. The truth was I was only at the apartment by in stretch because of his foul treatment of me.

The moments he did act like he cared wouldn't ever be enough to overshadow all of the bad. *I knew that*, and yet, I heard him out anyway. By the end of that call, I reluctantly agreed not to completely cut him out of my life, but I wasn't sure what that would look like. I can't explain why it was still so hard for me to let this guy go. I wish I could have.

When school started, my very first day, I bumped into him

on campus. He got on me for vaping and then had a quick, friendly moment with me before going to the food hall. His friendly moments never made me feel better because I still didn't feel like he was consistently there for me in the ways I needed him to be. I also hated not knowing if he could see me while walking around campus. I felt so insecure and ugly after everything in our history; I dreaded not being prepared for a random run-in with him.

I remember he'd text me occasionally, saying things like "I see you," and it would always make me uncomfortable with the unknowns of how I looked. I began to feel like I was under a microscope, even though there were limited times when he intentionally *tried* to see me. That was also hurtful in a weird way because it made me feel like the ball was in his court, but he didn't do much with it. I wished that he would have treated our friendship as though it were sacred all the time, not just when I was pushing him away.

The more time went on, I began to realize that I sucked at this whole one-foot-in-the-door thing. It wasn't like Charlie and I had some new falling out; I just couldn't handle the warped feelings that would arise with every interaction we had. Nothing was really okay for me, I just kept pretending it was. It was making me sick to my stomach to have him be so upbeat and jokey for these random 2-minute interactions; he would never ask me anything real.

I felt like I had gone through all of this pain and destruction at his hands, and yet, *he* was the one who came out the other side of it with peace. I began to loathe myself even more as I came to the horrific realization that I did all of this damage to my life for *nothing*. This "show" I put on to save face hadn't gotten me anywhere but further down a dark hole. I was the one who needed to find peace, but I still didn't know how. It all felt so unfair.

I began to start shaking after I'd get through moments of him casually talking to me for these short periods of time in passing. Even just seeing him on campus began to make me shake and feel nauseous whether we spoke or not. Too many feelings began to engulf my ability to breathe. I tried to avoid seeing him if I could help it at times. I'm sure he must have felt like I was bipolar if he picked up on that.

Go Fish

I continued to drink excessively at the apartment, and I even started skinny dipping in the community pool. I was the first to have the guts to do something that dumb, and then others we'd have over started to join in. Josie and I began to regain some semblance of a friendship in our drunken nights together, but she wasn't ever consistently around because she was seeing a different guy every couple of weeks.

I literally couldn't keep them all straight. I remember one night, I woke up to her having sex with a guy on her side of the room. I was thankful for my headphones, but it didn't make that any less awkward. Derek and I began to talk again, but I could tell that his guilt showed in every interaction we had for a while. I guess it would have been weird if he didn't feel remorse for his actions. We mostly played card games together when we'd hang out, even some as simple as Go Fish.

I learned that Pete was in a rehab center across the country, so I decided to take advantage of the distance and send him a peace-making message. I never dreamed what would happen next. All I said was I forgave him and hoped the best for him. He replied within two minutes and asked me to participate in his recovery journey. I told him I was okay to talk occasionally, considering the distance. He literally got a Greyhound ticket and arrived in town 48 hours later wanting to see me. Derek was angry at me for agreeing to see him. I didn't tell my family about this either because I was embarrassed that he returned to town after my impulsive move to reach out. That wasn't my intention at all! I still craved peace in my life, and since I wasn't going to have any lasting peace with Charlie, I was trying to grasp it wherever else I could.

I reluctantly met up with Pete a couple of days later. It was a peaceful, brief encounter...*or so I thought*. A few days after the night I saw him in person, I was being followed by an old burgundy sedan. I didn't recognize the girl in the driver's seat, but it was pretty apparent that Pete was on the passenger side. I was going to my parents' house, and when I pulled in, they slowed down and waited until I got out of the car. They flipped me off and yelled at me to go f*ck myself. I remember a furry took over within me as I ran up the driveway and cussed back at them...absolutely no care in the world for my parents' potential humiliation with that move.

I was only there to drop something off, so I left fairly quickly to get gas. Once I pulled into the gas station, I looked down at my phone and decided to call Pete out. He probably didn't think I knew it was him, and even though I couldn't see his face, I knew no one else was dumb enough to pull such a stupid stunt.

Besides, this was only 5 days after he had come home...*it had to be him*. Why would he do that after a peaceful encounter? No clue…but he had no problem being a bipolar psycho back when we were "together," so I didn't need to understand whatever twisted reasons were behind this nonsense. He would *not* come near my parents' house again without some serious hell from me.

So, I dialed him up, and he answered casually. I told him to listen well and called him a few demeaning, yet highly fitting names. He began to yell at me…he had never heard me talk to him like that before, and it was *long* overdue. I yelled over him in a condescending tone, told him to shut the f**k up and said if he ever followed me again or came within a square mile of my parents' house, I'd f**king kill him.

All I heard him yell was, "WHAT THE FU—" before I hung up on him. I didn't owe him anything and I didn't want to hear some made-up lie that it wasn't him. When it comes to manipulative people, even the most pathetic of them…you're still in charge of how much rope you give. You can choose not to give them any or give them just enough to hang themselves with. Pete was only ever able to manipulate me in the past because of how badly I hated myself.

I was grateful that he finally had the opportunity to see that I wasn't the same pathetic, weak girl from the summer before. It was as if Pete had just met me for the first time. I smiled as I looked at myself in my rearview mirror…I felt like I was finally getting my voice back.

Wake Up-Drink.

My older cousins from up north came down to stay with us and took me to a rock concert. We had never known each other much before this trip, but boy, did we bond while they were here. They got Josie and I into several bars downtown and bought us drinks every night; countless memories were made in those four days. I was worried about getting them in trouble at first (and us, of course), but after I'd get two or three drinks into the night, I was pretty much in a hakuna matata state of mind. I felt invincible to all the weight I was carrying. It was the most incredible time; all we did was sleep in, eat what we wanted, and go to places we had never been able to get into. They were fun, drama-free guys, and Derek and Josie immediately loved them.

My cousins being there brought the three of us together for a good time for a few days despite our differences and on and off disappointments with one another. The concert was also such a fun experience. I had learned that Ralph would be at the concert, but I had no idea he would be only a few rows down from me and my cousins.

With that arena's size, it was like a needle in a haystack chance that we'd even run into each other. I was grateful to continue being on good terms with him even though seeing him carried a bittersweet feeling. He seemed just as surprised and happy to see me as I was to see him, and we went and shared a cigarette during the break. I longed to go back in time to our first date. I would have clung on longer before embarking on our friendship if I'd known what was just around the corner for me. Never mind that now, I thought. *Just drink.* Just be happy. Little did my twenty-year-old self know, being drunk never equates to being truly happy.

The last night my cousins stayed with us, Derek drove me home from downtown, and Josie rode with them. We left a little before they did, and I remember some guys pulled over beside us and began yelling flirtatious things at me when we were at a red light.

Derek yelled back and floored it after them when the light turned green. They pulled over in front of us, and Derek did the same and proceeded to get out of the car, threatening them for saying stuff to me. He referred to me as "his girl." I kept begging him to get back in the car; I was so afraid something bad was going to happen.

When he finally got back in and shut the door, I remember staring at him. He finally asked me what I was staring at. I asked him what that was all about…considering I wasn't his girl, I didn't understand why he cared if some random guy said stuff to me. He replied, "They don't know you're not my girl." He said it with such a serious, straight face that I couldn't stop laughing at the whole thing after that.

When we got home, we sat in the car for a second singing and howling out "Animals" by Maroon 5. When the song ended, he leaned over and started kissing me. I don't know why, but I kissed him back…*a lot.* We went inside and continued making out in his bedroom until we heard the front door open. We played it off and acted super casual when everyone walked in. I was surprised that I found any enjoyment in kissing him after everything that had happened. I guess that wasn't too shocking considering my rap sheet of emotional chaos.

My cousins left the following day, and we all were sad to see them go.

Derek and I had another make-out session that got fairly heated about a week later. We had been drinking and swimming at the pool. I was wearing my suit this time, and so was he. We watched a movie in his bed and made out when Josie wasn't home. I wasn't too worried about it bothering her because she never cared one way or the other about my feelings initially. I also knew that Derek and I wouldn't sleep together because I couldn't bring myself to. I was too scared I'd end up with a disease after how many girls I'd seen him bring home just in the few months we lived together.

After that second time that we made out and fooled around, I think it offended him that I didn't sleep with him. I remember waking up the following day back in bed, relieved that I didn't cave in with how hot and heavy things got between us. I went to the bathroom and was immediately alarmed at the sight of my underwear…they were soaked in blood from his long nails when he had touched me, and it made me sick to my stomach.

Even without sleeping with him, I still felt so dirty inside from the emptiness that was eating away at my heart. I wasn't this girl…this girl that fooled around randomly. I caught a glance at myself in the mirror and began to feel almost unrecognizable from who I once was. I wished I could be myself again, but I felt so far away from who I used to be more than ever. The longer I kept running, the harder it was to stop.

I remember getting a call from Derek later that night. He asked me to pick him up down the road because he had been at a party and was drunk. So, I did. When I got there, he had a blonde chick that he was holding hands with behind his back. He didn't tell me I would be driving him and his next one-night stand home. He omitted that detail because he knew he had just been trying to have sex with me the night before. He proved my point and reasoning for not giving myself away at a new record. I was more grateful than ever that I didn't sleep with him.

Thankfully, I wasn't terribly hurt by it because I knew that this was to be expected with his history. I don't think he knew what to do with my kindness towards him and blondie on that seemingly long ride back. When we walked into the apartment, she went into his room with him, and I went into the kitchen to get something to drink. He entered the kitchen a moment later and tried to profess some half-a** apology. I shut the fridge door and made eye contact with him as I chuckled slightly. I told him that is why "this" (as I pointed back and forth between him and me) will never happen. I walked past him and shut my bedroom door.

Bitter Talks

It was now late September, and things at the apartment began to take a downturn again because Derek started letting his friends crash on our couch without running it by us. It didn't bother me much until Josie started sleeping with one of them; sharing a room with her made that uncomfortable. At that point, I had no space of my own because she was letting this hobo stay in our room. It wasn't that I hadn't had a "hobo experience" myself, but this was different. I didn't invade someone else's space when I went slumming.

Derek had also grown angry with me over his apparent bruised ego. I'm not sure he could ever justify being mad at me after what he did to my face. Nonetheless, he was acting like he hated my guts. The truth was, I hated his the more he acted entitled to be a prick towards me.

I was drunk and miserable in my room one night, and I decided to try and reach out to Charlie. We had been so distant at school, but I wanted to see if he would be there for me if he knew I wasn't okay. I was never vulnerable like that; I never legitimately asked for help from him or anyone. I just needed to get away from the apartment; getting high in such a toxic environment had lost its appeal.

I hesitated to push send, but in tears, I reluctantly did. He replied a couple of minutes later. He told me he couldn't come because he was sick and had no gas money. He added that he had faith in me to make better choices. I didn't reply. I felt so stupid for even texting him. The last thing I needed was his condescension.

In the following weeks, I grew more distant from Derek and Josie as school kept me busy and for other obvious reasons. I had also been hanging out with my other friends and going on random Tinder dates. Those were never great. When I was home, I participated in drinking mostly.

One night, the tension sparked between Derek and Josie over a dog that he brought home that did not get along well with her dog. Derek was highly ill-equipped to take care of him and kept yelling at him when he'd have an accident. I stayed with the pup all night. The poor thing was so dirty, and he didn't take to anyone but me. I feel sick to my stomach even thinking about it because I think Derek just dumped him on the side of the road a few days after taking him in. I prayed he ended up somewhere safe with a loving owner.

Not long after that, I came home to Josie and the same couch hobo in our room again. I didn't want to watch or listen to them having sex, so I went and sat in Derek's room with him. He had moved the TV in there out of spite a week or two earlier.

He was still angry with me for icing him out after the blonde chick situation. Earlier that night, he and I had a short conversation where he tried to make me sound like I had a low IQ. He acted like

I was beneath him and spoiled. I didn't say much in return when he first said that, but as the night went on, I realized that I'd had more than enough crap to contend with. I wasn't going to put up with anyone else trying to make me feel small.

We got into a big fight that became somewhat physical. It started when he told me to go back to my room. I yelled back at him that I couldn't because his hobo friend was in there boning Josie in my space. He said he didn't care and made some derogatory comment about me going to my parents' house. I smirked at that same old rebuttal and told him how I felt about his ungrateful a** in a less-than-quiet tone. He acted like I had a silver spoon in my mouth, and I was over it.

I pointed to every single nice piece of furniture in his room that his grandmother had purchased for him; furniture that he never so much as bothered to put together. I talked about the car he owned that I had helped him pay for when he was short on the downpayment; the same car he totaled within a few months of having it because he was likely drunk and/or high behind the wheel. I threw in his face how he's the one who gave up his full track scholarship and a world of opportunities after only a year. Every word I said was dripping in frustration with him, even though, the truth was, I was being a bit hypocritical. I too had destroyed so many opportunities for myself in my anguish and with the poor choices that followed. I wasn't so different from him at all when it came to my areas of self-sabotage.

He sat in silence with an angry look on his face, staring at the television. Feeling ignored pissed me off even more. I remember using my arm to swipe all of the empty beer bottles and trash off of this random folding table he had next to him; every bit of it went all over him and the bed. That triggered him to leap up and get on top of me, screaming back in my face. He was holding me down by my wrists, and I screamed right back at him, continuing to call him out on his bulls**t. I proceeded to kick his leg out from under him that had been holding him up. He bitterly got off of me and told me to get out.

We didn't speak for the rest of the night. The next day, I went into his room to get one of my DVDs after making myself some dinner. He was sitting in there in his chair. I looked around the room, and I couldn't believe it…the entirety of his bedroom was put together impeccably. There was not a piece of trash in sight. I told him it looked nice, and he muttered a thank you. After I grabbed the movie I was looking for, he grabbed my hand as I was walking away. He said, "Hey." I paused but didn't say anything as I looked at him. He didn't return eye contact, but a moment later, he said, "I love you." I told him I loved him too and squeezed his hand before letting go.

End of an Era

In the coming weeks, things unraveled completely at the apartment. Josie and Derek were constantly getting into fights. He continued to let people in and out of our apartment like it was a hostel, and he carried a gun with him and would take strange videos holding it up for social media. I was hardly there anymore, but when Josie told me that she was done and planning to walk out, I agreed to join her in making a meeting with the office to see our options. It made sense to call it before things got any worse.

The office said we had no way out of it. We explained that he was letting other people live in the apartment, causing structural damage, doing drugs, carrying an illegal weapon, and anything else that could help make the case for them to let us break this lease. After they continued saying there was nothing they could do, we finally said we'd refuse to pay anymore if they didn't provide us a way out.

They threatened the attachment of our wages if we were to do so. I laughed and invited them to take the rest of what filled my account…all .78 cents of it. I informed them that I had no current wages to attach. It was clear that they grew concerned that they wouldn't be able to get any money out of us without a big headache.

They reluctantly drafted the lease break paperwork but stated that we would obviously still need Derek's signature. We owed the lease break fees and damage fees from Derek's bedroom door he had busted up when he got angry one night. We were clueless as to what we could do to light a fire under Derek's butt to pay his portion of the fees, but thankfully he did sign the paperwork.

Unfortunately, as our move out deadline was approaching, Derek still hadn't paid his amount, nor had he moved a single thing out. We began to worry that we'd end up in a sticky situation if he didn't hold up his end. When we mentioned this to the leasing office, they recommended moving his furniture outside.

This advice was completely illegal and ridiculous. It would solve nothing. I told my parents what the leasing office told us to do with Derek's stuff, and they were appalled that they would give us illegal advice just to save them the trouble of kicking him out. We again informed Derek of our final amounts and told him we had to be officially moved out by December. We never heard anything back from him. I had moved out already, and so had Josie, so I'm sure it wasn't a surprise to him to receive a formal move-out date.

I remember Dad and I helping Josie move into her new apartment that she found for a great deal. It was a lot closer to her place of work. She and I had been on better terms lately. It almost felt like we were getting back to our friendship after the veil of the apartment was lifted. I'll admit, I was a little jealous that I didn't get to move out to my own apartment after she partially wrecked our first one, but ultimately, I was just grateful for the support my parents provided me. Moving back home was much needed.

I wanted to surprise Josie with the couch that she had purchased. I asked my dad if we could take the truck to pick it up. He agreed, and it wasn't a small ask because we had to carry it up three flights of stairs. We also bought her a Mini-Christmas tree and left it on her counter for her to come home to. She seemed touched that we did that for her and thanked us profusely when she came home from work to see everything all set up.

She had asked me if I wanted to move in with her at one point, but I kindly declined the invitation. I knew our friendship had been through enough hurdles and I just wanted to coast for a while. I needed to take some time to breathe and reset 'on my own' even though I was technically back home.

Less than a week after living in her new apartment, Josie had a very big surprise…she found out she was pregnant. I was so scared for her, and I knew she was freaking out. She didn't know what to do, and in her panic, she considered listening to the leasing office people. Derek was still at the apartment and had not moved a thing out the last time she went over there to check. Josie said that she tried talking to him with no luck and we both had sent him texts explaining that he needed to be out by the deadline. Josie was scared that we would end up having to pay his amount if he didn't get his stuff out of there and pay his portion.

We were all technically liable, so we started to wonder if he was intentionally trying to hurt us with this because of how everything went down. I remember her telling me that she was pretty set on getting some guys from work to help her move his stuff out, but I knew that would result in worse things for us. Especially her in her current condition. We could frankly be arrested for doing what the office had advised us to do.

I went to her work and tried to talk her out of it. I felt like she wasn't hearing me because she continued talking about her plans to dump his stuff outside. I raised my voice regarding her pregnancy and why that was the worst thing she could possibly do with all that she was facing. She looked at me with anger but hurt is what filled her eyes. I didn't mean to hurt her. No one was around us when I raised my voice about it, but I could tell it still made her feel ashamed.

She basically cut me out of her life after that conversation. I should have waited to talk to her until she wasn't at work, but I was scared that she'd do something she would end up regretting. Thankfully, Derek ended up moving out by the allotted timeline we were given from the leasing office. He paid his third for the break lease fee, and we were officially all free of each other.

Learning to Breathe

Even though I was technically free from a lot of the toxic stuff that had been holding me down, I felt more trapped within myself than ever. My anxiety came back with a vengeance once I moved back home. I guess the same thing happened the year before when I was officially free of all distractions and back in reality. It wasn't like I could drink much around my parents either, so there was no quick, easy escape from it all. I was so depressed and angry about everything. None of the "peace" I found was ever lasting. I knew I had looked for it in all of the wrong places, but I didn't know how to get back on track with all of my baggage.

It was now winter break, so at least I had a breather from having to avoid Charlie or, worse, having to save face with Charlie if there was no option to avoid him. I always say he was the flakey one, but I guess, in some ways, I was too. My ups and downs with him always felt like a protective mechanism; a response I deemed valid to his lack of sensitivity. I had days where I could smile through my hurt and hope for the ability to just let everything go, and other days where I knew pretending that this weird dynamic was fine with me was utterly stupid. Other times, I felt like I deserved the pain that was heaped on me by not drawing a definitive line in the sand and sticking with it.

Deep down, I understood that there wouldn't be any healing to come from someone so incapable of emotion; the times he had been so casually cruel were never forgotten. I was haunted by all of my memories; even the good ones had finally been engulfed by the reality of where they ultimately landed me. I always felt like a shell of myself walking around campus every day, and I wasn't doing that much better on the home front. Little by little, I was continuing to drift into an empty abyss. I had many moments where it felt like I was suffocating, and I remember I'd be up until 3 in the morning most nights trying to get past my debilitating anxiety. Tears would stream down my face as I was unable to get to a full breath. Sleeping pills ended up being the only way I could get any sleep for several weeks after I moved home.

I had rekindled with another friend from high school for New Year's (Sandy). I was trying to stay busy and force myself to white knuckle my rough days leading up to the end of the year. I ended up meeting this guy through Sandy and her cousin; he was my New Year's kiss that year. I had also gotten back in touch with one of my friends from Westwood named Kelsie. She was engaged, and her fiancé had a single friend who wanted to meet me. I went on some double dates with them and was also texting back and forth with the guy I met on New Year's.

I found some relief in having new faces in my life. People who didn't know my past and just filled my present with laughter. I had started spending a lot of time with Kelsie and her fiancé (Dean) and his friend, Tom. Tom was working his way up to becoming a police officer after spending 7 years in the military. He had sad eyes, but a gentle smile and he treated me with such kindness. When we kissed, I was sad to say that I didn't feel anything for him. The feelings just never sparked. I tried not to take advantage of his sweetness by being honest whenever he asked if I wanted to be more. I felt bad, but I knew that honesty was the best way, and frankly, the only way for me to move forward in my life.

Tom also had just gotten out of a relationship with a woman he had a baby with, so maybe there was a part of me that was afraid to get involved in something so complicated. Dean was a very flirtatious person, but I didn't really think much of that because he seemed to be that way with everybody. Dean and Kelsie were getting married just around the corner, and I was really happy for them. I carried some mixed emotions internally at the same time because I felt so far away from that chapter for myself.

I had always hoped to marry young and have children young. That seemed so out of reach for me as I continued to fight to get through each day with my anxiety and depression. The only comfort I found in my difficult mental state was that I didn't let it show. I was always on the go, and that seemed to be the one thing that kept the past from swallowing me up.

It helped that I eventually stopped running into Charlie on campus, but I still felt like I was always looking over my shoulder. I blamed him for my anxiety, losing Westwood, losing myself...*everything* really. We never texted again after the last night I reached out for help, and he didn't show up. Time away from him always brought me the most healing after experiencing the way he treated the opportunities he had with me back in his life. And having new people in my circle began to help my mind stay in the moment. I was very grateful for that.

A Rock and a Hard Place

I remember being invited to go four-wheeling with Kelsie, Dean, and Tom. I never turned down any opportunities to get myself out of the house, especially not on this particular day. Today was January 10th, and the last place I wanted to be was alone. The night had been fun all throughout and was much like every time we got together. It was exactly what I needed to stay afloat and not dwell on the past.

As nightfall came, we decided to start a bonfire and hang out in the woods for a while before heading home. I remember that this was the first time I ever drank a beer and enjoyed it. They had brought some vodka and some Land Shark. We split everything up amongst each other and took turns taking swigs of the vodka.

The night had been pretty spectacular, and I remember feeling grateful to have friends in my life again. When it started getting late, we decided to say our goodbyes. I had planned to go back with Tom to stay at his place on his pullout couch to avoid potentially drinking and driving. Tom hadn't consumed much at all because of the stomach condition he developed in the military. After we finished cleaning up, we went to hug one another. I had already hugged Kelsie goodbye, so she was in the truck waiting for Dean.

When Dean went in to hug me, he kissed me instead. I pushed him back. I couldn't believe what he had just done. I didn't say a word, but I knew it was very likely that Kelsie had just seen him do that. I felt so sick over it, even though it wasn't my fault. They were literally about to get married…I didn't know what the hell was the matter with him?! She was five feet away from us when he did that, so now I could only imagine what else he did when she wasn't around.

I told Tom when I got into the truck what happened, and I was freaking out. He said that maybe it was just an accident and maybe Kelsie didn't see anything. It was pretty obvious that Kelsie had seen. We were following behind them to drop off some of the stuff at Dean's, and their car swerved and came to a complete stop at one point. When we got back to Dean's mom's house where they were temporarily staying, Kelsie went in without saying a word. I had to pee, so I nervously went inside, hoping that she'd talk to me. She didn't. She went into Dean's room and shut the door behind her. I didn't know what to do. I was devastated that he would do something so stupid. I wondered if she blamed me for it somehow…I reacted as quickly as I could. I had never been flirtatious back with him in an inappropriate way, but I was always friendly.

Of course, now, all I could do was think over every interaction we'd ever had, trying to make sense of why he'd feel like he could just come up and kiss me like that. With the timing of their wedding, I kept hoping that it was a total accident…we had all been drinking, and maybe he was just not thinking clearly. I spent the night in a tailspin over this, and I talked Tom's ear off about it. When we were sitting on his porch, he finally told me that, sadly, this wasn't Dean's first time acting like this. He had an apparent history of letting his flirtatious behavior get the better of him. Tom never elaborated, but that helped me put any guilt or second-guessing I had to rest. I still felt terrible for Kelsie, but I didn't know what to do.

The following morning, I left rather early. It was about a 45-minute drive home, and when I was about twenty minutes away, I received a text from Dean. He apologized for the kiss and said that he was drunk and didn't mean it. I accepted his apology and told him I wanted to never speak of it again.

The following week, we all hung out again to go to this concert they had an extra ticket for. Ironically, the guy that I met on New Year's Eve (Blake) was taking his dad to the same concert. I was so relieved that Kelsie was talking to me again and grateful nothing came up about the stupid kiss. We found our seats in the arena, and I remember I got a message from Blake that he could see me from where he was sitting.

I looked up to my right and saw him waving beside his dad. I waved back, and we agreed to go meet up in the main area. Tom came with me and took a picture of us and then joined in for one. It was painfully obvious that Tom was getting wasted; I had never seen him intoxicated because I thought his medical condition wouldn't allow him to drink excessively without some serious repercussions. Apparently, that didn't matter to him on this particular night. Being drunk isn't flattering on anyone, but it's especially unappealing when it's someone you don't share the same feelings for.

After we said bye to Blake and moved back to our seats, Tom began to act very strangely. He began intentionally running into me on my side and making my beer spill. He did it about 20 times and thought it was hilarious. Dean and Keslie seemed to notice that he was getting pretty drunk and offered to put him in the middle so he wouldn't keep ramming me into the sidebars. Blake even noticed how rough Tom was being and offered to make room for me by him and his dad if I wanted to sit with them. I told him I appreciated the offer but chose to stay where I was.

After the concert, I had a party I had to go to for a friend who had just moved into her apartment. On the way back to my car, Kelsie had sat with me in the backseat because Tom was still pretty tweaked. We were goofing around listening to music, and the song "I Kissed a Girl" came on. We put on a quick two-second show for Dean and Tom in the backseat. I had never kissed a girl before; it wasn't my thing. I'm not really sure why we chose to do that, but it almost felt like Kelsie was showing off for Dean.

Between the two of them, it seemed only right that she receive the last kiss in my numbed out mind. After they dropped me in the driveway, I remember being irritated that Dean picked me up when he hugged me goodbye. I felt like he was really pushing it with Kelsie by even hugging me at all. That was the last time that I remember spending time with them because not long after that night, I ended up in a relationship with Blake.

A New Toad

Blake and I started seeing each other even though he didn't live nearby. He lived a little over an hour away and we only saw each other on weekends mostly. The first time we got close was when he came to stay with his older brother up at State, and they invited me to come by. I got along with his brother and his friends pretty well. I remember his brother seemed to take to me when I knew all the words to this Lil Dicky song; he thought it was hilarious. I didn't stay the night that night even though they made me feel more than welcome. I just wanted to get to know Blake more before I did anything like that.

I ended up staying the night when I went up to his place for his birthday a few weeks later. I bought us some steaks, potatoes, and a cake and we grilled out together. It felt like such a special night. I was really starting to like him because he seemed so genuine. He also didn't push me for sex; he just held me all night long.

The second time he came down to stay with his brother, I stayed the night there with him. I remember being mortified that I didn't plan well enough to bring deodorant. I was borrowing his brother's shirt to sleep in, and I felt like I had major BO. Gross.

He came by the house the next day and met my parents, and we watched a movie before he drove home. I was never a big fan of long distance, but he texted me or Snapchatted me so frequently that it never felt like we really skipped a beat. We weren't officially dating yet, but I started to feel like I could see myself with him. My mom felt that he was odd the first time she met him. She wanted to find out what types of food he liked so she could cook for him if he ever came back by. His response was cold and almost uninterested in reciprocating the kindness my mom was extending. My grandfather didn't seem to care for him much either. Blake was always sweet to me in the beginning, but I didn't pay attention (big surprise) to some of his seemingly off-color attributes.

What can I say? I was addicted to distractions and a-holes.

We had a massive snowstorm about a week after he had met my parents. Everything was frozen, and I hadn't left the house in two days. Even if I didn't have a rear-wheel-drive situation to contend with, I probably wouldn't have gone anywhere just because ice and brakes don't mix well with any vehicle choice. However, in addition to his day job, Blake was a volunteer firefighter and felt that he was enough of a dare-devil to come and get me with a couple of his friends in their truck.

He was living with them after his house got wrecked by a fallen tree in the same wide-spread snowstorm. I thought it was so endearing that he had lived on his great-grandparent's property and that he was close to them. I had always been so close to mine and hoped to find someone who shared the same values as me. I was sad about his house; it was cute, just needed a little fixing, and I felt like I was a million miles away from all of my sadness when I'd come visit him there. I wasn't sure I'd have that same feeling in his friend's home, but thankfully, they were nice and made me feel welcome. They were engaged and getting married in late spring.

I remember they gave me a wedding invitation that I found rather odd. It was apparently an inside joke regarding how many people Blake had slept with since he and his long-time girlfriend had split up. It said to "Blakes New Whore" or something like that. I initially didn't get the impression that he slept around a lot. He was on the heavier side, and even though he was tall, he wasn't exactly what you would call a "looker."

In all honesty, when I first laid eyes on him on New Year's Eve, I literally thought to myself, "Dang, it's a fat guy." I know…totally terrible to judge someone like that. It was after getting to know him that I ended up finding him charming. He seemed like a sweet guy, and he made me laugh. But not long after we started getting involved, he admitted to me that he was known for being an a**hole. And I didn't listen. *Shocker.*

I remember their little volunteer firefighter walkie-talkies going off in the early morning hours and I would wait in bed while they'd respond. And when I say bed, I mean a floor pallet. He didn't have a room set up yet, so we were just sleeping on the living room floor. I had brought my schoolwork up there so I could get some stuff done when they'd be out on calls. I also went to the fire department and hung out with everyone there. While they were all very nice, it became clear after a short period of time that Blake had brought a lot of girls around.

In addition to that red flag, he also had a lip ring. The ring wasn't what bothered me, but the fact that he'd take it out before church to cover it up made me feel like he wasn't as real as he claimed to be. He was also in a panic on Sundays about his grandma finding out that I was staying with him. Obviously, I'd never go around bragging about that. I started to see that he put out a lot of smoke and mirrors, and it should have occurred to me that he was likely doing that with me, too.

At the time, we still hadn't had sex. He was so tender and loving towards me. He'd take me out, or we'd stay home, but either way, he showed me a good time. I was a cheap date; I pretty much only ate appetizers everywhere we went. And if we stayed in, I was always very content to drink whiskey and cuddle. But after a little over a month of us spending every weekend together, I felt weird not knowing what this was. It was during the week that I was snowed in with him that I finally asked if we were ever going to be a label. He told me that he had been planning to take me out into the freshly fallen snow to ask me properly to be his girl. I thought that was cute, and I actually felt bad that I ruined his plan to ask me out formally.

He seemed to take our relationship very seriously; he kept talking about marriage and life goals with me on a regular basis. Topics that most guys avoid for quite some time seemed to be at the forefront of his mind and desires. His initiating of those conversations made me feel close to him quicker than I expected.

I noticed that he was very concerned about my 'well-being,' and when I wasn't with him, he was constantly checking up on me. If he saw a different background in a Snap I'd send him, he'd immediately ask where I was and stuff like that. I could tell beneath the surface he was insecure, and frankly, so was I. But I thought we were in this together, so I wasn't worried. I took the insecurities he had and interpreted them as him being protective of me.

We had already been tossing the L word at one another after only knowing each other for about 6 weeks. After dinner one night, I let him take me to bed. I hadn't slept with anyone in over a year and a half…not since Pete. He was shocked that I'd not been with anyone in that long. I told him I was holding out because, truthfully, I was. I was trying to get back onto my path. The path where I met a loving Christian guy who wanted to carve out a life with me, have babies and love me so purely that I could forget *everything else*. I wanted to be free of all of my emptiness. I wanted the family life that I had always dreamed of and to see my parents at peace; they deserved to know that I was going to be okay.

While I was so eager to embark on that chapter, I was still so young. I was only 21 at this point, and I didn't realize that it was okay to just be 21. God's plans for me didn't require rushing. But I wanted to stay in the fast lane, even though somewhere inside, I knew something was off. The morning after we had sex, things began to change. He stopped getting my door for me. He started to be cruder and was quick to try and make me feel bad in conversations. I would wake up covered in bruises after we'd have sex, mainly on my boobs. I didn't know what I liked in bed because I had never had much of a normal experience. I just wanted to be loved, and I held onto the hope that he really did love me for the next couple of months until we imploded.

I will say there's a reason God says to do things His way. I kept getting hurt trying to do it mine.

We used to go out on Fridays and Saturdays with his friends to this hot spot outside of town where the drinks were cheap, and the music was decent. We'd drink and dance the night away, and that made my past feel so far from me that I could truly smile again. However, Blake's insecurities started to make going out a little on the stressful side.

There were nights that he'd get so jealous if a guy even looked at me. He'd get in guy's faces and then take me out of wherever we were. It was odd to me that he had not grown to trust me at all, but his possessive behavior aided in my insecurities a bit, too. It felt good that he cared, even though sometimes the behavior he'd exert was a bit much. But then, something else came about that put me in a strange place with our relationship.

He came up to me one night when we were taking a break from dancing and told me to look over at the bar at this girl sitting there. He said that she worked at the chiropractic office he had been going to, and that she had been hitting on him. (I know, super weird that my 22-year-old boyfriend was going to the chiropractor…what can I say? The guy was literally broken down at 22. Another red flag I ignored.) I asked him if she knew that he was taken. He said that he had told her that, but she was still persistently trying to get his attention.

I didn't know where he was going with this, so my confident version of myself kicked in and explained to him that if I had to deal with that (I pointed in her direction discreetly), we'd no longer be a going concern. He seemed to register what I was saying. I moved on with my night and continued dancing with everyone. In the back of my mind, I knew a guy who truly loved me would have handled that situation rather than telling me about a potential continuation of it.

In the coming weeks, we began to get worse and worse. Not only did he not put that situation to rest with the one girl, but there was another girl at the chiropractic office who was apparently pining for him as well. The girls were close friends. I actually spoke with them on a few different occasions when we'd be out dancing; I kept things friendly even though I thought the dynamic of their friendship and their intentions were odd to say the least.

Blake and I ended up breaking up fairly quickly after that. I think he wanted me to be the jealous type; he seemed to take offense that I didn't try to engage these girls in an ugly way. I also think he found a much more suitable match. He ended up with the second girl that had been pining for him. I'm not sure exactly how that worked out with the initial girl and her being friends, but I found it funny. While I wasn't initially relieved by our breakup, ultimately, I was so grateful. If I were to run into them today, I'd hug his now wife because her pursuits saved me from what could have been a life that just wasn't for me. There's a lid to every pot, and he definitely wasn't mine.

After we split, I was able to look at everything for what it really was…and it was awful. Blake was a racist and ugly-hearted person. (At least back then…perhaps things changed). I learned a lot about him in the last couple of weeks we were together, and I had begun to put my walls up as he continued revealing more of his true colors. For example, I recall being at breakfast one morning, and he literally told his friends that I wouldn't let him put "it" in my butt. He was a degenerate hick that would often say crude things like that. He also used to hit his friend's dogs at random when they'd try to jump up on the couch with us. He did it so casually and frequently. It infuriated me and made me not want to be around him. And when I say 'hit', I mean closed fist hitting these dogs in the face.

Another disgusting thing he said to me once was how if we ever had children together, they weren't going to be allowed to date black people. I couldn't even wrap my brain around why he'd say something so prejudiced. I made sure to let him know that I had lived with and loved a black guy, and some of my closest friends were black, so he was going to have to get over that weirdness or depart from me. Being from the West Coast, I was always so shocked to come across anyone who was genuinely racist. I just didn't grow up around that at all.

Needless to say, we both parted from one another without regrets. I think we both knew we couldn't build the life we wanted with each other because we were just too different in the head and in the heart. The last day we were together, he had been fairly ugly towards me, and I told him that he should be careful not to mistake my kindness for weakness. Even though my remark seemed lost on him, I was still proud that I didn't let his treatment of me go unchecked before I walked away. I was slowly but surely getting my voice back every time that I finally took a stand or walked away from toxicity.

Thankfully, that relationship was very short-lived, and I got out of there without getting pregnant or getting an STD. I remember not long after we started sleeping together, he began to threaten that he'd sleep with the very next girl he met at a bar if I ever cheated on him or dumped him. They always say that those who talk like that are oftentimes the cheaters themselves, and I guess he proved that theory to be accurate. The second chiropractor girl moved in with him nine days after we broke up according to his friends. They had messaged me that they missed me the first night they all went out after the breakup without me. I'll be honest…I missed his friends the most. They were my favorite distraction.

I mended my loneliness fairly quickly when I rekindled with Ralph again. He always offered up a bar stool beside him if I needed to get out and laugh a little. The truth was, I had that with my mom every day; we always found ways to laugh at our hardships together. I could tell that she was *so* grateful that things didn't work out with Blake. She had been worried I'd end up pregnant and stuck out there in the boonies with him. I was relieved for that, too. If I hadn't had her, I wouldn't have made it through any of the things I went through. I was still holding my head up high in the midst of feeling low because she truly saw *me* when I no longer could. She still does.

Learning to See

Sometime prior to the breakup, I remember Charlie saw me on campus from afar. It was early in the morning, and there was no one around us because classes had already begun. I was running late and rushing to get out of the cold and into the building. I heard Charlie call out for me and I stopped and turned around. I paused for a moment, but thinking of Blake and how happy I finally thought I was, I turned around and kept going. I know that was probably strange to Charlie because I had never blatantly ignored him like that before, but I wanted to move on with my life. I didn't want the past to come up and swallow me anymore. Besides, it wasn't like we had ever had a consistent friendship outside of temporal moments that sprung from a "forgiveness" that lacked any real ownership of the past events.

Even after the breakup, I didn't regret being done with Charlie. I just wished that it had helped me as much as I thought it would. I still saw him off and on when I'd be walking to my classes, and I struggled with the same problems I'd had before. I couldn't control the shaking and nausea that accompanied each sighting. In some ways, it was worse now because I felt rejected and hurt by yet another person I had finally allowed myself to be vulnerable with.

Word to the wise: when someone warns you they're an a**hole, listen to them. And in general, when people show you who they are, always believe what's right in front of you. Not what "potential" you think they have. I had spent so much of my life at that point only seeing people through this hopeful lens when their true character was typically always right in front of me.

Ralph and I spent a lot of time together, and I found relief in seeing him. I even told him the truth about what happened with Charlie one night when I had been struggling with severe anxiety. He was there for me even though he knew my feelings for Charlie had developed when we were still together. I was grateful for his forgiveness and his warmth. His family would let me stay the night on their couch if I ever stayed out late with them, and I began to feel a sense of calm back in my life.

I felt sad thinking back on how I walked away from Ralph more than ever. He was a nice guy and had I just rode things out longer with him, maybe none of the bad would have ever happened. We were better off as friends, but I just remember kicking myself, thinking back on the timeline of how things unfolded. I even developed a bit of a newfound crush on him because of his tenderness towards me during this chapter.

Eventually, I felt like I was ready to start looking around at apartments again. But this time, I wanted to live alone. I was reluctant to let Mom and Dad pay for my rent, but they once again insisted that a dorm situation wouldn't be much different.

Additionally, State was a quarter of the cost of Westwood, so my schooling budget afforded me more wiggle room. I decided to get a job against my mother's will to try and at least pay for my gas, car insurance, utilities, and groceries.

I ended up meeting a sweet girl at my favorite local bar who recommended I come to work at this dealership she worked at. Dad helped me sharpen up my resume, and I applied for the job; I scored it the following day after dropping off my information. I remember that I was so excited to have a fresh start. I had just moved into my new place, and I was feeling optimistic about the future.

I was still drinking fairly heavily, but I was working 30 hours a week and doing 16 hours with school and crushing both. I continued to struggle off and on with anxiety and depression, but between my job and school, I had enough to keep pushing myself forward so that I didn't stay down for long stretches of time. I went home a lot and spent time with my parents and my grandfather, which always lifted my spirits.

I went out on several dates and never really felt connected to anyone that I dated. I was a little sad about that because I ultimately still longed for something deep. Everyone around me was so content with the temporal, but I always wanted to plant roots and dive into life. Yet, I was still making out with practically everyone I met when I'd go partying downtown or at my favorite local spot. It made me feel empty and far away from my dreams the more I partook in fleeting nights like that.

I rekindled with Jamie after what I'd call a "sabbatical" in our friendship. I decided to forgive him for talking about my private stuff because I missed him. I wanted someone around who knew the old me; I craved the comfort of familiarity when everyone new ended up being disappointing in one way or another. I had also continued to avoid Charlie at school even though there was still a part of me that wished things didn't have to be so broken and messed up.

I knew avoiding him was the right thing to do, but I still struggled with leaving it all unchecked. He would sometimes wave at me if he saw me, and on a couple of occasions, I instinctually waved back too. Sadly, I continued to have involuntary shakes and a racing heart, and I resented that the past still had such a strong grip on me. After all the time that had passed, I didn't really understand why…I guess seeing him just brought up too many painful memories. Reality never lined up with the peace I hoped to find in my odd predicament. And nothing I ever did in regard to him felt right; I always felt like I was just permanently trapped in some foreign, strange place with no real resolve.

I remember I would drive angry all the time. It's a miracle I never killed myself or someone else with how reckless I was. I would blare my music as loud as it would go; chills would overtake my arms and behind my neck as the lyrics and the bass would attempt to reach the depths of the anguish I felt in my heart. I wanted to scream, but I let my engine do it instead. I never had a single speeding ticket, but I camped out near three digits on my speedometer far too often. I likely would have lost my license if I'd ever been caught, and I would have deserved it. The days I had to go to campus seemed to fuel my lead foot the most.

The cold fronts I put up toward Charlie probably didn't really register with him because he was such a disconnected person. He still probably felt that he could come in and out of my life as he pleased under the notion that "all was supposedly forgiven." I had not make a formal declaration about him leaving me alone…I just hoped my body language and the fact that we hadn't spoken in a year conveyed that I was uninterested in rekindling. I didn't see the need for some random, dramatic conversation about it. Frankly, I hoped I would just grow strong enough to not care one way or another if I saw him or not.

I regretted choosing to go to school at State. I felt like I made a huge mistake because I knew the main reason I applied there was to prove to Charlie that I was fine. And I wasn't…I still wasn't fine at all…not even almost 3 years later.

I would have days where I was doing fantastic with work, and enjoying my new apartment, but then all it would take was a sighting at school to send my mind into a tailspin. It would affect me beyond the realms of the campus at times which was disheartening for me. I could be in a crowd of people and still feel completely alone, drowning in the memories of 2013. I would try to drink away all of the things I couldn't change on my bad nights. Nights when new distractions just weren't enough to calm the old voices in my head. I wish I had realized that facing all of it and calling things what they were was the only way to climb out of that dark pit. Doing well at work, in school, and every other area of my life wouldn't fix something that was still so profoundly broken inside.

During all of my sleepless nights, I would reflect back on everything, wishing I'd had more dignity…wishing that I'd been smarter. I still tried to hold onto the good memories whenever songs or random things would trigger me so that the bad ones wouldn't take me down. I even tried to maintain some forgiveness from a distance, hoping to be released from some of it somehow. It was hard when I carried so much underlying anger and resentment towards Charlie, though. The weirdest part was how I couldn't ever fully bring myself to legitimately *hate* him; *I* was the only one I truly hated.

I guess that was the ultimate proof that he didn't take away every good part of me; my heart was still intact, even with how hard I tried to numb it. I just needed to learn how to love myself again. But in order to do that, I would need to understand that I had *always* been loved and that God could still make *all things new* in my life if I'd let Him. This stain did not need to define me.

One late, lonely night, I said a prayer for the first time in a long time out loud in my room as if Jesus was sitting on the edge of my bed with me. I just remember asking Him to help me start finding peace right where I was in my life. I also prayed that he'd send me a good guy. Someone who would love me right and bring healing to my scars.

The Dealership

I was beginning to find a lot of happiness at work. It had its stressful days, but I worked with a great team of people, and I really craved having the busy environment to keep me going. I remember my first day of work when I was formally introduced to everybody…I didn't know it, but I shook my future husband's hand. It was now the end of September in 2015, and I felt like my feet were finally touching the ground again. Between work, school, hanging out with my family, and trying to see my friends on occasion, I was practically on the go every day of the week. My past began to slowly fade into the background of my new life more and more with every passing day. I felt like I was finally doing it right, and I was actually proud of myself. I stopped avoiding my reflection in the mirror, and I even started praying regularly again.

A couple of months later, on a random busy Saturday, I felt my heart drop into my stomach when I looked at the list of customers who had made purchases on vehicles that day. I saw Charlie's dad's name on the list. I immediately asked one of the other girls I worked with (Gigi) if he had been in the dealership that day because I didn't remember seeing him. I had been running around like a crazy person doing a hundred other tasks. Gigi said that he had been standing off to the left for a couple of hours earlier that day, waiting for finance to call him back for paperwork.

I felt sick at the thought of not knowing if he saw me and if he would tell Charlie where I worked. I was afraid of having any more surprises. Having to see Charlie at school was already hard on me, but the thought of him showing up in my new space where I was finally embarking on a better path made me nervous. I really wanted everything I had begun to carve out for myself to remain sacred and untainted by my past. It seemed extreme to assume he would end up coming to the dealership in some ways, but I knew that Charlie still worked for his dad, and it was likely a work vehicle that he had purchased. I was uncomfortable with the unknowns of the whole situation. I dropped the subject and tried not to think about it.

A week later, everything I had feared came true. I remember walking out of the bathroom, and as I was rounding the corner, I saw a woman and her son standing in the cashier line. I told her that we had a kid's playroom if her son wanted to play in there while she was waiting to pay. Right as I began to walk away, Charlie appeared with a hat in front of her and said my name. I turned around when I heard him, and I'm sure my face looked just as frazzled as I felt.

I had been cold towards him on campus, hadn't spoken to him in over a year, and even if that wasn't enough of a clue that I didn't want him to approach me, my reaction towards him surely got the point across. I asked him what he was doing here, and as he began to talk about picking up the vehicle, I cut him off, saying,

"Yeah, the transit van. I saw it on our records. Why are *you* picking it up?" He said that his dad asked him to. I began to back away after his response and told him I had to go.

When I got back to the front desk, Gigi could in see my face that something was wrong. I told her not to look back because I didn't want Charlie to make any assumptions. I still had this need that I can't explain to never let him see me vulnerable; he couldn't know he had that kind of power over me. I had never smoked at work before, and I knew that Martin (my future husband) smoked, so I went and asked him for a cigarette after clearing it with Gigi and the owner.

It was a very busy day and, frankly, the worst time for me to take a smoke break, but I just had to get out of there for a minute. Gigi didn't know the details, but I briefly told her enough so she wouldn't think I was just acting like a mental case or trying to leave her with all of the clientele. She was so kind to me about it; she hooked her arm in mine and walked with me past Charlie, towards the back of the building. I didn't ask her to, but I was so grateful she helped me bypass another potentially awful moment.

I sat out there and tried to calm my nerves with each puff. When I looked out in front of me by the service doors, I saw an old beat-up GMC that I didn't recognize. Right as the strange vehicle placement caught my eye, I saw Charlie walking over to it. I looked away and down at my phone as my heart started racing. I heard the truck start. Right as it began to pull away, he must have seen me because he ended up just moving the truck into a parking spot before approaching me.

He casually took a seat at the table I was sitting at. My efforts to exert space between us were lost on him, and I took some blame upon myself for that based on my past actions. I don't remember what we discussed in the small talk he tried to make with me, but I kept it brief. I saw a customer out on the lot, so I put the cigarette out and told him I had to go. As I made my way down the aisles of cars, I felt like my legs were visibly shaking. I tried to talk, and it felt like a lump the size of a baseball had formed around my voice box. Each word was a struggle, and I just hoped that the man I spoke to would assume it was the cold chill in the air that accounted for the shakiness in my voice.

When I finally went back into the building, I was still shaken up. I knew that I needed to snap out of it and get back into work mode. I approached the desk, and I heard the owner calling for me. When I went into his office, he asked me if I was okay in light of the random smoke break I asked for on such a busy day. I didn't want him to think that I was slacking off, so after he asked me to sit down for a minute, I answered him honestly. I told him that I didn't mean to make a drama out of it, but there was someone who had hurt me in the past that came into the dealership, and I unexpectedly ran into them. He asked what I meant by "hurt", and I told him the PG version. I said the word "assault" rather than rape to avoid dumping such a harsh word into the conversation. He seemed to care for my well-being and said that if he ever came back into the dealership, I should let him know.

I felt a little awkward for sharing something so personal, but I was touched that a few people had my back in the workplace. I had never had that before. It wasn't until a year after being married to my husband that I learned he had also gone looking for me outside that day; he said he could tell when I asked him for a cigarette that something was off. Our paths never crossed that day, but it meant a lot to me that he cared enough to leave the desk with how busy they were to check on me. I remember how badly I wanted to preserve this chapter and savor the feeling of freeing myself from my past. I knew I couldn't control if Charlie were to pop up in my life, but I felt relieved that I was able to handle that situation on the spot as well as I did that day.

I had plans to go out downtown with some of the girls for my 22nd birthday that night, and boy, was I ready to drink after the day I'd had. I didn't get into the details, but I did tell Carmen briefly how Charlie showed up at my work and cornered me. We stayed out until almost 3 A.M., but thankfully I didn't have to be work at until noon the next day. I thought that would give me ample time to recover from the night before. It was only a 6-hour shift, so I figured I had it covered, but it ended up being a long, long day with that hangover.

An Onion

A few days later, the girl who introduced me to this job came over to my apartment. We had a couple of drinks before thinking about the ingredients I would need to cook us dinner; I had everything I needed apart from an onion. On our way to the store, I offered to let her drive my car because she said she'd never driven a Camero before. That was a big mistake. I didn't realize she was intoxicated because I wasn't paying attention, and I personally didn't feel buzzed at all.

Long story short, she wrecked my car on a curb going 40mph. My door wouldn't open because the undercarriage of the fender was smashed in underneath, blocking it from being able to open. After I climbed out my passenger window, I noticed that my rim was destroyed, too. I called my dad, and thankfully, he showed up right away. I didn't know how much this was going to cost, but I knew my friend was a single mom who didn't need to be spending her money fixing this mess that was frankly just as much on me as it was on her. Neither of us should have had drinks and driven anywhere. So, because of the grace and kindness my parents extended, I didn't need to get insurance involved. I told my boss about it the next day, and they towed my car into the shop for free. I was very grateful.

Being stuck without a ride was difficult, especially with how far away the campus was. I had to get rides to work and borrow my parent's truck to get to and from campus the two days a week I had classes. My car was set to be in the shop for a couple of weeks. I was so embarrassed, and I felt terrible about all of it. I had to ask for rides from various people because I wasn't going to ask my parents to come to and from that side of town twice a day, 3 times a week, in addition to borrowing the truck for school.

One night, I got a ride home from a couple of the salesmen that I had gotten to know a little at work. We stopped and got a drink at the local bar I usually frequented. I was hesitant to hang out with any of the guys from work because I really didn't want to jeopardize or ruin my job if anything were to ever happen in a drunken haze. I didn't find anyone attractive except for Martin, who was technically one of my managers, though I didn't report to him directly. The number one rule my hiring manager told me during my first week was that we were not allowed to date anyone at the dealership. I didn't want to risk anything by toying around with that rule.

Out of everyone at work, Martin had actually been the first one to reach out to me outside of the work setting; he friended me on Facebook after I got the job. He seemed like a sweet guy, but I knew he had kids, and I later learned that he was going through a divorce. Complicated. Not for me, I thought. But curiosity got the better of me as I sat there at the bar with the salesmen from work receiving messages from him. Martin and I had spoken a couple times before via messenger, and he had invited me to come over if I ever wanted to have a bonfire with him. I kept things friendly and open even though I was internally a bit closed off because of all he was going through and my concerns for my job.

I finally asked the guys what they knew of him and if he was a good guy. Being that he was their direct manager, I didn't know what they'd have to say. However, both of them immediately said that he was a great guy without any hesitation; they had nothing but nice things to say about his character, too. I absorbed that, but I knew his situation would be too much for me. The truth was, I had begun to give up on finding anyone during this chapter of my life; it seemed like the more I dated, the more I realized everyone was all the same.

That night when the guys dropped me off at my apartment, they came upstairs to see my place for a few minutes only to prove the accuracy of my thoughts on everyone's desires being both singular and typical. They had both been smoking weed and drinking, so it was entirely stupid on my part to invite them in at all. They had always been really nice, and I felt decently comfortable with them up until this point. When we were sitting on the couch, one of them started to undo my pants. He started touching the top lacy part of my underwear while he was simultaneously attempting to kiss me. I told him that I couldn't do that and began pushing him away as I said it was time for them to go. Thankfully, the other one piped up immediately and said the same thing. He texted me and apologized for the other guy being so abrupt, and I appreciated his kindness.

While I was grateful things didn't end badly that night, it now felt too awkward to ask them for a ride. I decided that I would reach out to Martin and see if he wouldn't mind getting me because my apartment wasn't too far off the highway. From our minimal conversations, I knew that he would be driving in my direction anyway, and I hoped that would make it less inconvenient. He replied that it was no problem at all. I offered to treat him to a beer to thank him for giving me a ride, and we tentatively planned for the weekend. He and I ended up meeting up on his side of town, which was also near my parents' place.

I wasn't nervous to see him because, in my mind, I knew that we obviously would never be anything more than friendly coworkers. He was one of my managers, after all. His piercing green eyes and adorable smile did turn my head now and then at work, but my mind was still so focused on keeping things straightforward in my life.

He barely spoke the night that we first met up for a drink. I felt like I did all of the talking outside of him showing me some pictures of some wood pieces he had worked on and some pictures of his son who I thought was absolutely adorable. He also talked about this property that was for sale that he wanted to buy so he could build a workshop on it and do more carpentry work for a side hustle. I laughed because I knew exactly which property he was talking about. In fact, I had been on that property a few times with my ex from high school and his cousins playing laser tag because it was next door to his grandparent's house.

After we called it a night, he walked me out and gave me a hug by my dad's truck that he graciously lent to me for the evening. He smelled good, and his hug felt incredible, but us being a thing still never even entered my radar that night.

The R Word

About a week later, I got my keys back from the shop, and I no longer had to ask everyone for rides. It felt so good to have my freedom back. I had a few more days of classes before winter break would ensue, and I had some big exams coming up that I needed to prepare for. I was retaking one of the classes I had failed at Westwood back when I was giving up on life, and I was still struggling to understand the material.

I was so frustrated with myself, but I made a last-ditch effort to retype my whole study guide and read through all of my notes for the billionth time. All of a sudden, everything clicked. It was the first and only time that I ever truly loved science. I remember acing that final exam and being overjoyed by my ability to have a successful redo. I also remember wishing that life could be that simple in every area.

It was around that time that I also recalled seeing Charlie on campus again. He was playing his guitar and singing right out front of the library, where I had to walk to get to my other classes. While I was feeling proud of myself for the first time in a long time, it was clear that the devil was trying to drag me back into apprehension.

Feelings of failure and sadness began to erode my newfound smile that day. And that was it. Something inside me was just done carrying around these feelings of unworthiness. It was time that I truly called things what they were, no matter what the result may be. *One. Last. Time.* But not like before. This time, I wasn't going to send a little message or a text. I decided I wasn't going to give him any wiggle room to water down what he had done in some back and forth discussion. I was going to say the word loud and clear.

I remember sitting at home later that night, drinking one of the vodka mixers I used to make. I needed a little liquid courage to push me to say everything *exactly* how it happened. And I did. I sent him two separate recordings. One was 6 minutes long, and the other was 3. I left nothing unsaid in those messages; they covered the ins and outs of everything I felt, why I reacted the way I did to his actions, and why the aftermath became so detrimental and messy for me.

I was done pretending like I was fine. I explained to him how all of the dominos that fell in my life in the last three years began with him and were now ending with me. I told him that I gave him so many opportunities to truly try and be there for me and own what he did. I even chose to be transparent with how stupid I felt for ever thinking he could help bring me healing with what a disconnected person he was. I was every vulnerable thing I had been afraid to be in those recordings.

I called him out on everything from January 10th, 2013, all the way up to him recently dropping in on me at work. I said the word rape without hesitation and broke down the definition of rape so there'd be no more "confusion" over what he had done. I reiterated the very words I had said to him in the back of the truck when I was shakily trying to push him off, saying, "Charlie, I can't do this." I refreshed his memory of his despicable response, "We already are." I didn't leave a single detail out of that moment, even down to the cold smile he gave me as he ignored my plea for him to stop as he finished.

I wanted that night to be burned into his memory the way that it was irrevocably burned into mine. I told him how hard I fought to get myself to a better place and how I wouldn't let him ruin that for me. I made it clear that I expected him to make no mistake in understanding me now that I was saying this loud and clear…he was to stay away from me. I also told him that he should seek out some professional help.

I felt immense relief after sending those over to him. Drunk or not, everything I said was one hundred percent accurate and had needed to be said and *heard* for three long years. The next morning, I had to be at work early for my twelve-hour shift. I dressed nicer than normal, wore darker makeup, and put myself together more than I had in quite a while. Speaking the truth lifted such an incredible weight off my shoulders.

I told my mom what I had done, and she was proud of me for standing up for myself. I could also hear in her voice how sick all of this made her. I had hoped that through this decision, I could finally put this matter to rest. My family deserved peace. I wanted them to see me thrive beyond the nightmare that had been consuming so much of my heart for so long. It was definitely part of my reasoning for wanting to have the courage to call him out one final time.

Forgiveness and Fallen Tears

It was around 9 A.M. when I began receiving texts from Charlie in response to my recordings. He was once again not how I expected. It reminded me of the first and, frankly, the only time that I truly called him out. Instead of being ugly or defensive, he seemed to own it. He told me that he had admitted everything that he had done to his dad. He said that he was no longer welcome at his dad's house because of what he admitted to doing to his stepsister when they were kids. They had cut him off in every area apart from paying for his therapy. Again, this was the last thing that I expected to hear him say.

I told him that I was glad that he was getting help. From there, he instantly dove into wanting to see me to 'make this right' with us. He told me that he wanted me to be able to look him in the eyes as he told me how sorry he was for everything…

So here I was, thinking that I had just done the very thing I had been avoiding for years. The right thing. The brave thing. The thing that would finally cut Charlie out of my life for good. I always thought if I were to say it all out loud the way I had that, I would never have to see him again because I figured he'd steer as far away from me as possible. And then he dropped this response on me. I didn't know what to say.

I thought about the potential vindication I had already had without knowing it now that he was finally being honest with his family. I felt my guard come down a little just on that fact alone. I wondered about his therapy…the prognosis, and the details of what went on in his messed-up head. I continued pondering all of this, sitting in my office chair as more texts from him came flying in.

I began to contemplate what this would do for me. He said, "The hell with waiting anymore. Let's meet right now." I had never received a full-on, real apology from him in the past. He never *fully* admitted to anything, nor did he own his cruelties in the aftermath of the rape. I wanted that very much, even if it was meaningless in the scheme of what was already done. Even if he was too damaged to ever change whatever was so warped and twisted within him. I wanted to hear him say it. I felt like I deserved that much. So, I agreed to see him.

He wanted to meet up immediately, and I guess I did too in some ways, but I had to tell him that I was working until 8 o'clock that night. We made plans to meet up afterward at Starbucks downtown, about 15 minutes from my work. He said he'd have a friend give him a ride and be waiting for him in the car while we talked. I knew that was more for his protection, and I understood his desire to stay above reproach.

I felt relieved at the thought of finally hearing him own this; I had lost hope that the day would ever come when he would. I wondered if I'd feel more whole again if he admitted the truth and gave me as genuine of an apology as he was capable of. I didn't know if he'd ever be able to have a full and complete understanding of everything and the ramifications that came from what he had done; I just knew I had to find out if any relief could come from all of this.

That night, we had a dealer tag missing, so I was running late because Martin and I were trying to find it. We were the only ones left in the whole building, and it was a big deal to lose one of those. It was getting late, and I was already running 20 minutes behind. Martin knew that I had plans, so he offered to keep looking for a few minutes before calling it a night. He told me he'd text me if he found it; he figured one of the salesmen just left it on the back of a vehicle.

I was grateful that he offered to keep looking for me. I had been so anxious about this talk with Charlie all day; I felt like I would burst if I had to delay it another minute. I wanted to just get it over with because a big part of me was scared to do it at all. Everything with Charlie had been like a nasty combination of quicksand and kryptonite for so long…I prayed that this talk could finally put that to an end for me.

When I got there, it was freezing outside. I parked in the parking garage and came around the corner to see Charlie sitting there in the cold at a two-seater table with no jacket on. He was shivering so badly that it was hard to understand him, and he laughed, knowing he sounded terrible. I didn't know that Starbucks closed at 8, and I told him that I would have met him somewhere else. He said it was okay and that he was just so happy I agreed to meet with him. I knew his friend was waiting in the car a few yards away, so I felt fine to offer for us to sit in mine and talk where it was warm. He agreed, as the heater was very persuasive.

When we got in, he shared his relief to be out of the cold before a blanket of silence covered us for a couple of minutes. I just stared at my steering wheel and waited for him to talk first. I remember him beginning by telling me how the guilt of what he did to his sister led him to open up to his dad. I sat there listening to how his family reacted to this news and how no one would speak to him apart from his father anymore.

He also said that his dad had fired him prior to him making his confession because of an accident he caused with one of their work vehicles. Charlie said that he had been really fighting to keep closer to God more than ever because he felt like his whole life was imploding and there was nowhere left to go but up at this point. I remained quiet and finally looked over at him when he asked me about us. He wanted me to tell him everything from my perspective that happened on January 10th, 2013.

I was hesitant to at first because I realized that he never told his family about what he had done to me or anyone else. I thought his text said that he had confessed *everything* to his dad. It turns out that it was just stuff with his sister. That must have been much worse than what he had told Jamie and me because, from what he had shared with us, it was nothing more than childlike curiosity. Things I had experienced myself when I was a kid. That didn't make it okay, but it didn't seem sinister in how he described it.

Of course, after my experiences with him, maybe it was best to let him call himself out. If he confessed it and was exiled over it, then it must have been worse than he let on. I still wondered if what happened with his grandfather had something to do with all of it; surely, if that were true, it was a driving factor. I sat there thinking about everything and decided to swallow my disappointment that he didn't confess a word of what he had done to me. The only person I really wanted vindication from was him, anyway.

I took a deep breath and began telling him everything through my eyes. It was a strange feeling telling someone about events that they were a part of. He had already heard the worst of it in the recordings that I sent, but I went over the whole night from beginning to end. I wondered if he would cut me off, try to argue with me, or defend himself, but he didn't do any of that. He just sat there, and after I began to get into the details of the backseat, he reached over for my hand.

I didn't move away, but I didn't hold onto him either; I just let my hand remain limp as he cradled it within both of his. By the time I finished telling him the story of the darkest night of my life, I felt his tears landing on my hand. He began to sob softly as I finished telling him what became of me internally after that night and how I felt like I had lost pieces of myself in that darkness that I couldn't ever seem to get back. I remember him kissing my hand as his tears continued to fall. I could tell there was a sincerity that I had never seen in him before. It genuinely seemed like it was the first time that he realized what he had done.

In a broken voice, I heard him tell me how sorry he was. I still didn't say anything; I couldn't believe that I was getting a real apology from him after all this time. One that seemed to come from so deep within his heart that it was somehow able to touch mine.

When he asked if I could ever forgive him, I sat there and looked into his eyes. The eyes that had once gone so black and cold on me in the most vulnerable moment of my life. Eyes that once were truly unrecognizable from the friend that I thought I knew and loved. I could see a glimpse of the person I saw in him back when our friendship was in its purest form. All of these split-second clips of memories of us flooded my mind and my heart as I held his gaze.

I forgive you.

He immediately reached to put his arms around me, and we hugged for a long time. I was amazed at the relief I felt. They say that forgiving someone is necessary for you to move forward, whether they ever verbalize an apology or not. I will say having them say it out loud makes a whole world of difference. I was grateful for this moment…this moment that I never thought I'd have.

I dropped him off at his friend's car, and we went our separate ways. He sent me a text that I read upon arriving back at my apartment. He shared his thankfulness for me agreeing to see him, and then he told me that he felt like the greatest weight had been lifted off of him. I said the same in return. We both decided that we wanted to rekindle with Jamie for old times' sake now that we had decided to formally move past this.

I knew that this would be the strangest dinner to plan, and I didn't really know what to expect from it. I also knew that while the forgiveness that had finally taken place with Charlie was real, the best way to preserve it would be to not spend too much time together. I wanted to keep things as sacred as possible going forward, and from what I could tell, Charlie did, too.

Every Little Thing's Gonna Be Alright

I noticed that Charlie still exerted extremely socially awkward behaviors. We had made plans to hang out once prior to our dinner with Jamie, and I was surprised that some things never changed with him. I picked him up to go get a coffee and talk, but we ended up just doing a drive instead. He was nearly out of gas and didn't have a check coming in for another couple of days, so I offered to do the driving.

When we were in the car, he squirted all of the perfume I carried in my purse everywhere intentionally and was loud and obnoxious like he used to be. It wasn't like I expected everything to change, but I didn't expect him to act that openly weird around me after the depths we had just crawled out of. It didn't discourage me from the dinner because I still felt like that would be a good thing for the three of us, as bizarre as it was. However, it did make me feel confident about the internal decision I had made to preserve what was good by not carving out too much time to see him. He was still an odd individual, but I felt like I had found peace with him in spite of the past.

A couple of days later, Martin and I decided to go out for beers again. I had asked him a week prior, and he had plans, so he asked me if I was free on Saturday. I remember feeling hesitant the night that I went to meet up with him. It was just the usual feeling of wanting to make sure I didn't do anything to jeopardize my job or make anything weird at work. I was also embarrassed because I was wearing the same outfit that I wore the first night that we'd ever hung out outside of work. He asked if I'd meet him at a local bar that was on my parents' side of town. It was a little further out than the one we had met at the first time, but still close. When I walked in, I saw him sitting at the bar on the far side, talking to some guy. He looked really handsome. He always looked good, but I had never seen him not in his work clothes. I sat next to him, and he ordered me a drink.

At first, our conversation was light and vacant of anything fundamental, but that didn't last for long. We began talking about everything under the sun, and I think we were both surprised to find how much we had in common. He was ten years older than me, with two kids, and two different moms. He had been through hell, and so had I. I think that's what ultimately made us fall for each other so quickly; we both had jagged edges that somehow fit together.

Martin truly has one of the biggest hearts of anyone I've ever known. I had already begun to see glimpses of his heart at work when I saw how he always went the extra mile with the way he treated others. He also had a strong work ethic that stood out amongst everyone else. Both of those things really mattered to me, but I tried to remain conscious of the fact that his personal life was fairly complex.

As I said, I'd been on countless dates and kissed many frogs prior to meeting Martin, but there was not one that made me feel a thing. That's why I never dreamed that I'd feel something so strong for someone so complicated by the time he leaned in to kiss me. I had been hoping he would the more time we spent talking that night…there was something so tender and real about him that captivated me.

The feeling of falling in love is a transcendent experience, better than any high. I remember us talking until the bar closed around 2:30 in the morning. We ended up continuing the night (early morning) in his truck because we couldn't seem to break away from this new beautiful thing we had just stumbled into. We just wanted to know everything about one another, and of course, we kissed every moment in between finding out. I loved his hands. They were such masculine hands that seemed like they could truly hold onto me and never let me go.

It was raining so hard, and he really didn't want me to drive home in the storm. He offered up his spare bedroom and said I could stay the night if I wanted. I didn't want to drive home in the storm either, but I knew it was the right thing to do. I was afraid with how connected I felt to this guy that I'd end up sleeping with him, and I didn't want to ruin anything between us. In the back of my mind, I also didn't know him well enough to know if he'd have regrets about this in the morning. What if he lost his job over us being this close? He had kids, for crying out loud…kids…plural!! I was beginning to sober up from the spell on his lips when I realized what this could mean for his situation…and mine. I told him I had to go.

The next morning, I wasn't sure what to expect. I had let him know that I made it home safely that night as he asked, but I wanted to keep things open for him to backpedal. After all, he had way more at stake than I did with his job. When he came into work, we had to pretend like we hadn't gotten fairly well acquainted the night before, but thankfully we did a pretty good job of it. After work, he texted me that he wanted to see me. I'll never forget when he arrived at my door…I might as well have been drooling when I first laid my eyes on him. It has been over 8 years, and I still remember him standing in the doorway of my apartment as if it were yesterday.

He was so dreamy. As he stood there smiling at me, I could tell that he had no regrets in what we had shared the night before. When we embraced for a hug, his touch made me weak at the knees. (I know that's an overused, cheesy thing to say, but it was the truth.) The way he held onto me felt different…unlike anything I had ever experienced. And the way his lips felt against mine was nothing short of beautiful. He had told me the night before that he was falling in love with me, and now, I couldn't deny that I was feeling the same. At the time, I still didn't know that forever was in the realm of possibilities for us, but I hoped that somehow, we could make all that we were feeling into something lasting.

We spent all night talking, and even after he went home, we talked on the phone until morning. The next day, at work, we pretended again, but we realized that we wouldn't be able to keep this a secret for too long if it continued. I couldn't stop staring at him. Lucky for him, he was able to see me discretely through two-way glass. My neck was getting sore from turning at every opportunity I had to look his way. That night after work, he came by, and we decided to go look at Christmas lights together at the same hotel that I'd been to with Charlie for his birthday three years before. It felt so good to make new memories there, even though I had gained a newfound forgiveness with Charlie.

I remember getting ready to go out with Martin that night…I was nervous, and I kept trying to tell myself it was just a date…nothing serious. It was an outright lie I was trying to tell myself in case this was all just going to end up being a massive letdown. After we pulled out of my apartment complex, he reached over for my hand; my hand felt safe in his. When we got there, Martin parked on the back lot, and we made our way through the hotel, taking in the incredible views together.

It felt surreal to be in such a special place with someone who really seemed to like me for who I was. He was such a gentleman, and he seemed so selflessly interested in getting to know me with no strings attached. We ended up sitting at this bar next to a beautiful indoor waterfall. We talked and talked and talked. I couldn't get enough of him, and he seemed to feel the same way about me. Each kiss felt more special than the last. The way he looked at me made me feel like I was already his to love. I kept thinking someone would pinch me, and I'd wake up to find that this was just a dream.

He kept taking pictures of me and of us. I began to feel like we'd been together for years the way we carried on. The best part of all of it was how he seemed so content just being with *me*. I felt like I was enough for the first time in…well, *ever.* He ended up asking one of the hotel receptionists for room pricing. He came up to me after speaking with her and asked me if I wanted to stay there with him so we could keep talking with the sounds and view of the waterfall in the background all night long.

I was so taken with him, and nothing about the idea of that scared me; it was just the opposite…I felt like I belonged with him. It sounds so crazy to say this, but through the conversations we'd had over just a few days, this man began to feel like *home* to me. I didn't even hesitate to say yes when he asked me. The only thing I shared reluctance about was how fancy the hotel was…I knew it had to be so expensive for him to do that for us, but he insisted that it was worth it to him.

When we got into the room, the blissful moments between us continued until we finally passed out around 3 in the morning. Right before we fell asleep, he said my name, and he told me that he had fallen in love with me. I told him the same, even though in the back of my mind, I was scared about his kids. I hadn't met them yet, and I knew if we didn't mesh, I couldn't be this person in the way of his relationship with them. I was so young. But nonetheless, I followed my heart, and I said I loved him back with every fiber of my being. As I lay there being held by this man, clothes and all, I began to feel like he was a true gift from God, and everything I had been praying for.

I awoke the next morning to a familiar sound. Martin's alarm was a song. It was the very same song that Charlie had sung that day we got stuck in the mud on the way to the store to get stuff for my mom to make dinner- "Three Little Birds" by Bob Marley. I felt this strange sense of peace come over me when I heard it because I felt like I could finally hear that song and be happy again; *every little thing finally did feel alright.* It didn't haunt me anymore, and neither did a hundred other things that used to get under my skin at random times. I was on cloud nine with Martin, and I felt so safe in my bubble with him.

The Love Contract

We decided that we needed to tell our boss and our managers about us when we got to work the next day. We casually told the owner that we needed a quick word with him. I had told Martin that I could just put in my notice and get a job somewhere else, but he wouldn't hear of it. He said he wasn't worried about his job. Thankfully, when we told our boss, while he was surprised, he didn't really skip a beat with just getting the necessary paperwork filed regarding our relationship. HR drafted what they called a "love contract" for both of us and all we had to do was sign. It was basically a piece of paper saying that Martin couldn't show me favoritism and we couldn't show open affection during work hours. No big deal.

My manager thought I was kidding when I first told her, but then she got on board. She laughed, knowing that I not only ended up dating someone from work, but I literally began dating one of the sales managers, of all people. So crazy, but one hundred percent genuine and real amid all the future unknowns. Things between Martin and I remained kosher at work, and we were able to keep our relationship discreet at first. It only took a couple of weeks for everyone to get wind that we were together though. Most everyone was happy for us, but there were a couple of people who cast their judgments. People who knew little of our situation and made false presumptions or shared unwanted opinions regarding our age gap.

My parents had the same age gap minus a year, got engaged quickly, and managed to stay together despite judgments from others, too (now 32 years and counting). The kids were the only thing that gave me pause when it came to our future, and for all the right reasons. I knew meeting them could change everything if they didn't like me, and I prepared myself for the worst in the back of my mind.

He had to pick up his son the night after we stayed at the hotel, so we didn't get to see each other after work. We talked on the phone until nearly five in the morning, even when we had to be at work at 8 A.M. We just couldn't stop talking to one another every moment we weren't together. And I loved it. Feeling so wanted made me feel things I never thought I'd ever feel after being in such a dark place. It may sound cheesy to say, but I really felt as though I'd found my other half. He even set my contact name as my initials with his last name.

Of course, I had this dinner thing coming up with Charlie and Jamie. I knew that I'd have to tell Martin the whole story for that to even begin to make sense, and even then, I didn't expect him to understand. It was going to be a strange send-off to our friendship, to say the least. I don't think that Charlie understood that I intended it to be a sendoff, either. I wasn't planning to "cut him out" of my life again, but I just knew I wouldn't have time or room to hang out like we used to with how quickly I was falling in love with someone so complex. My free time, as I knew it, would be slim to none. I also knew in my heart that it was better for us to only see one another in small doses to maintain this new path we were on.

I remember being nervous that I could lose Martin when I decided to tell him everything; I didn't want him to think I was a crazy person. Thankfully, he showed me understanding and respected my need to finish this the way I had planned before becoming an "us."

The night the guys came by, I was cooking sauce for some pasta. It was weird having the three of us together again, and yet, we seemed to pick up where we left off in some ways. Jamie had told me he had one condition with agreeing to let Charlie hang out with us again. He said if he ever caused me any more bruises with his rough play, he'd address it and not in the nicest of ways. I appreciated that. I still didn't understand why he was more protective over the least of the pains that Charlie had inflicted on me, but I accepted his kind intentions anyway.

They hung out with me in the kitchen while I cooked, each of us sipping a beer. I remember I was glowing with happiness over finding Martin; I couldn't stop gushing about him. Charlie piped up and asked if they were allowed to be "protective" over me when it came to him. I laughed and said, I guess, even though that dynamic was too odd for me to imagine. After I filled them in on everything, we ate and talked a bit about what Jamie had been up to, and then Charlie talked about work and school. The night ended quicker than I expected, but I was grateful that it had been good all the way around.

Charlie was still a little obnoxious (as I always knew to expect); he sprayed me with my sink nozzle when I had my back turned at one point while I was tending to the sauce. I had to change because I was soaked. It was like he had some weird compulsion to be a hyper 5-year-old. Despite that awkward moment, I still deemed the night a success in that I found peace. And it was enough peace for me to move forward in my new chapter with Martin.

A couple of days after the dinner, Martin surprised me with a gift that meant a lot to me. He bought me a cross that said, "It is well with my soul." He seemed to understand the significance of me being able to put this matter to rest in my heart, and I was so grateful to be able to share that joy with him. I was ready to embrace our future together and officially let the past go. I felt like I was finally free and like happiness was in my reach for the first time in 3 years. The tenderness in Martin's love was unlike anything I had ever experienced; I prayed I'd get to embark on forever with him now that I had broken away from this darkness.

Diving in

Martin technically never formally proposed to me…he just told me that he was going to marry me one day the night we stayed at the hotel. It wasn't even something that came up in a questionable sense; it was as if forever had already been decided by both of us. This love was so unexpected which made it feel even more special and God sent. I met both of the kids within weeks of that magical night, and everything felt so right with them too; I couldn't believe they accepted me so quickly. I wasn't sure how that would go, especially with his daughter. That basically sealed the deal with my only hesitancy.

Martin asked my dad for my hand. It wasn't exactly the prettiest of pictures for my parents to swallow…me marrying someone with two kids at 22 was frankly crazy. I am thankful to say they didn't brush him off despite how bad we looked together on paper. They took time to get to know him, and they saw what a big heart he had. But they also saw things that I didn't see back then because I was so consumed with my love for him. They noticed how much he drank. I guess I didn't really notice or care much because I still drank a lot, too. I knew that we both had started drinking heavily for different reasons, but my chains had finally begun to fall away from me as I dove into my new life with him. Sadly, Martin's chains did not.

Martin had gone to a party when he was 19. He unknowingly fathered a child at this party. The mother neglected to say anything until she and her family needed government aid to take care of this child, which was about 3 and half years later. My husband had moved to the city a couple of hours away from his hometown and was about to get married to a girl he met and fell in love with there. He was only 21 at the time when he got a letter in the mail requesting a DNA sample for a paternity test; he was one of two potential fathers. At 21, Martin had already begun to make a career for himself; he owned his own home and was persevering far beyond the depressing childhood he was once running from. Upon discovering that he was the father of this little girl, my husband fought with everything he had to have her in his life.

He had grown up in a broken home, and no one on either side of his family showed up to support him when he was in court fighting for his parental rights. Not even his newlywed wife who had initially claimed that she would support him in this battle and would accept his daughter as her own if he were to be granted shared custody.

The state saw how much money he made and spared no mercy on the monthly child support costs, even when he lost his job in the process of fighting for his daughter. The car business didn't allow the needed time off for this court battle, but once again, he made the right choice and continued fighting anyway. The amount of child support he was required to pay was enough for nearly two mortgage payments in his hometown. Sadly, his daughter's mother would use the majority of that money on drugs while leaving their daughter in the care of her parents.

The mom's parents did everything they could to poison Martin's relationship with his daughter. Based on ugly statements said in court, it was clear they resented that he was granted any parental rights at all. In addition to losing his job from all the driving back and forth for court in his home state, he also lost 27 thousand dollars (his life savings) in attorney's fees and eventually his marriage just to have his own daughter in his life.

While his wife had initially agreed to support him in this journey prior to their marriage, she changed her mind not long after he was granted shared custody. She couldn't handle the heaviness of the situation and began to phase out of her commitment to him while he was traveling back and forth, trying to build a relationship with his daughter on weekends. My husband said he'd do it all again, even if only to show his daughter that she was both loved and wanted.

Martin told me that he began drinking more after the divorce, and about a year after it was finalized, he met a woman that he knew from work who drank him under the table. He had heard some not-so-pleasant rumors about her, but at the time, he let the alcohol blind him to those negative attributes. Martin's friends mostly consisted of drunks who neglected to tell him some of the more violent and unstable things they had heard about her. Some of them even had first-hand experience with this woman's behavioral problems and still said nothing for years. While Martin's lack of discernment played a big role in this relationship, "true friends" look out for each other and should always be forthcoming of such vital information.

They got pregnant a few months into seeing each other and decided to get married about a year after their son was born. Through a bumpy few years, Martin continued to try and make it work for their son's sake until one day, he came home to find another man in his house. According to rumors, that was not the first affair she had on Martin. However, since there was no denying this one, that unpleasant encounter became the end of their marriage. Five months later, he and I met and fell in love.

I began to have a deep empathy for Martin the more I heard his story. Little to no family support, attempts to do the right thing against all odds, always to no avail, a poisoned well with his firstborn, and severe betrayal in his relationships. It was no wonder he drank as heavily as he did, I thought. His friends all seemed so kind and loving when I first met them, but time proved them to be just as disappointing as everything else. No one in his life was truly loyal, nor did they have his best interests at heart.

I wanted to save him from all of it. I wanted us to choose better, be better, live better, and prove everyone wrong. I knew life could be so beautiful for us if we would only choose to cling to what was good. But sadly, for a very, very long time, we did not. I think part of why we didn't adjust or change anything was because we never had any problems keeping up with our lives from our perspective. My husband always held down a good job, we never missed anything important for the kids, and we were active parents who got out there and showed up without alcohol present. But at the end of every day, we always drank from the time any of our commitments were done until we went to sleep. When I saw how badly that was beginning to hurt us, it woke me up.

To back track, we got married eight months after we got together. My parents pulled some amazing strings to get us into their rental so my stepson could go to one of the best public schools in the area. We were very grateful to them for letting us live there; they only charged us the mortgage rather than what they could have been making off of the property rent-wise. Martin took a job that would provide him more time with all of us, especially his daughter as she still lived two hours away in his hometown. I quit school temporarily to go back to work to supplement our income until his pay was set to improve.

Thankfully, I only took off two semesters and was able to finish my final five classes upon returning within one semester. I went through hell to finish because my guidance counselor neglected to tell me that I needed to spread some of my final core classes out because the workloads were too intense to take simultaneously. My professors all told me I was guaranteed to fail if I was taking just two of those three core classes I had signed up for. Not only was I taking all three, but I was also taking a math course I had put off (I suck at math) and an additional needed criminal justice credit through one of the toughest professors I'd had in the past.

I was in such despair at the thought of spreading my classes out amongst yet *another* semester, but I really didn't want to waste the money if I flunked out like they were all saying I was guaranteed to do. I was nearing the end of my first day as I walked into my Constitutional Issues class; I was heavily contemplating which classes I needed to drop and sought out some advice. My professor for that class was the only one who had a different opinion from all the rest, and he is the reason I chose to push on against the odds.

I not only passed, but I ended up with primarily A's and B's. I couldn't believe it. Every stressful moment of those past 5 months had paid off. I battled the flu twice and stayed up until midnight or later most nights for projects or in preparation for tests; I even found myself running on campus to get some of my hard-copy assignments printed and turned in on time. It was one of the proudest moments I'd had in years when I walked across the stage to receive my diploma.

Resentments and Trenches

Despite some of those amazing triumphs, things were fairly rough at home. My husband and I were constantly dealing with drunken late-night battles via phone with my stepson's mother and her boyfriend. There were some funds that she got in the divorce that were supposed to be used to pay off their past debts; it was laid out clearly in the Martial Dissolution Agreement, but she refused to pay it. Fees accumulated, letters were sent threatening to garnish our wages, etc. It was such a horrifically stressful time for about three years with this matter, and any other petty thing that could possibly come up between all of us had that tension fueling it.

Additionally, they refused to consistently show up for my stepson because it impacted their drinking time. That caused a lot of unpleasant conversations as well; I began to wage a war against them for disrupting the peace in our home with their ugliness. I pushed for us to hire an attorney after years of finding no resolve, and that seemed to put a large portion of the nonsense to rest seeing as documentation doesn't lie. However, even after finding relief monetarily with my husband's ex, the parenting situation (or lack thereof) planted a bitter seed in my heart. I was very quick to be ugly when prompted because I couldn't understand their selfishness when it came to our son.

Even his basic needs were considered an imposition it

seemed; I had to take him to every doctor and dentist appointment for years because it was never a priority to his own mother. She didn't even care to have him on Mother's Day the first few years that we were married because of how far out they moved. We always offered to meet halfway and she still passed on the idea several times or forgot the holiday altogether. This move was so irrational being that their jobs and our son's school were in the same town we lived in. It was clear that the only reason they moved an hour away was to own a bigger home. This distance made it to where our son had to be in the car for two hours every weekday just to get to school half the time. So unfair, and ridiculous.

On top of that heaviness, my husband and I had difficulty in conceiving children ourselves. He had a vasectomy for obvious reasons when he was married to my stepson's mother. Unfortunately, the reversal was not very successful in light of scar tissue. Knowing how easily my husband had been able to impregnate two of the worst mothers he could have possibly been with was like torture to my heart and mind. Especially considering how much slack I was having to pick up regarding my stepson daily.

He dealt with a lot of behavioral and cognitive issues that I believed were due to his mother's alcohol use during her pregnancy. This was another area that I felt very alone in as I attempted to nurture him to a better place. Other contributing factors with his negative behaviors spurred from the way his mom and her boyfriend would spoil him to avoid parenting. They made it to where he never had to lift a finger on their time, nor did he ever have to earn or want for anything. He was always extremely disrespectful towards his mom because of this unfortunate combination, and it would go unaddressed.

At our house, we held him accountable for his actions, made him clean up after himself, and we made him earn privileges. Having him only half the time left a lot of room for him to think he was an entitled prince. I will say, my stepson did a pretty amazing job of adjusting to the vast differences between the households after a couple years of our consistency thankfully.

I loved this kid, but I was still in a world of pain with my deepest desires feeling so far away. All I had ever wanted was to have kids (kids I didn't have to share with such awful people), and I feared that it might not ever happen for us the longer and harder the roads became. It's safe to say that the word "devastation" didn't even come close to covering the island of hurt and unknowns I was trapped in during those years.

In spite of all of that, there were these pockets of good throughout all of it that kept me going. About four months after we married, I remember my stepson asking if he could call me, "mom." I was so touched from the depths of my heart that he felt that connected to me, even with how hard I had to be on him at times. I took that role very seriously. Although they never married, my stepson's mom told him to call her boyfriend 'daddy' from the moment he moved in. I was grateful that wasn't the case with us; it meant so much more to me that he *chose* to call me mom. It was one of the hardest things I had ever signed up for in my life, but I truly love being a stepmom. I was too young to take on so much, but I was an old soul who genuinely put all of my heart into my family. My favorite times were when we had both kids with us.

Making memories with them made the sting of all the unpleasantries with their moms barrable. It certainly wasn't the life I imagined for myself, but on those days when we were all together and happy, I felt like it was actually even better. My fears and emptiness would feel far from me. My husband wouldn't drink much, if at all, when my stepdaughter was home with us, so that's also probably why those memories were even more special. He was one hundred percent present.

On the flip side of the good days, the ups and downs with both kid's moms were extremely stressful and almost became debilitating. Especially since my husband always took out his frustrations on himself, not realizing how that negatively impacted all of us. It affected me mostly as I took on the role of a buffer; it felt like I was constantly filling cracks at every turn, and the ones that were too big for me to fill caused such desolation in our relationship. I grew to resent my husband over the years for his drinking; his need to 'escape' made me feel like I was always having to face everything on my own. And what hurt the most was the fact that none of those stresses belonged to me. I chose to dive into the madness of his life with him and it felt like he would often abandon me in the middle of the storms.

I wanted us to find healing and prosper through all of the bad, but it seemed that he wanted to stay in the trenches every time things got tough on us. For years, he fought me on every good thing I tried to bring to the table, and the loneliness I felt in that kept me in a very dark place. What made it even worse was how he'd initially agree with the direction I wanted to take things, but he just wouldn't follow up with the actions on his part. It left me in the position of being a 'nag' in his mind, even though I just was trying to uphold stuff we 'agreed on' for the sake of our family.

I wrote a poem during one of the darkest times in our marriage when I felt like he truly didn't love me or the life we had built together. It encapsulated everything that I was presently feeling as well as a heaviness that I'd unknowingly still been harboring from my past.

Sip and Smile

The taste of the wine

Calms all the unanswered questions

It calms all the whys

The things that time was supposed to heal

The things my faith should have been able to override

They become inconsequential

Only for a moment in my mind

He looks at me and sees only the pain

He only sees the rainy days

The days where I stupidly tried to save him

As he added to my shame

With each sip, I remember

I remember my heart dying in vain

Maybe I'm the real hypocrite

The one who really can't let go

Of all the dark days that somehow used to feel like home

My twisted search and aching to feel whole

Maybe I'm not so innocent

What if I'm ultimately to blame

Will this bottle help me to face

That it was me who made the biggest mistake

Trusting in someone who would forsake me in the greatest of ways

I once believed that the best was yet to come

But how could that be

There is so much that can't be undone

These sips make me foggy

Yet somehow they set me free

Free of the misery of all I can't unsee

NINETEEN UNSAID

A prison of melancholy memories

Reliving my choice not to fight

The night the first domino fell

Little did I know

It was my first step into hell

Oh how consuming was my loathing

It's quite a dark process

Becoming that of a shell

A part of you left permanently roaming

With no one you can truly tell

I lay open and exposed

Remembering the timing and the words that once captivated me

Was I just that easy

I thought I finally found a home

A safe place to call my own

But this time I ignored all the red flags I was shown

A new darkness I must accept

For I had no idea just how dark was this life that I led

Until flickers of His light began to break in

My demons shouting and screaming

Made it hard to hear the whisper

The whisper telling me I still hold meaning

Was I blind when he touched me in the beginning

Was it the liquor on my lips that made my body feel like I was made for him

And his was made for me

Should I have left well enough alone

Should I have waited until I was fully grown

All of these things, I will never know

My hopes for healing have proven empty

NINETEEN UNSAID

Always fleeting and temporary

I am left feeling unworthy

Yet I still pray for a remedy

Meanwhile you're out there

Living your best life from where I stand

Do you treasure each moment

Knowing that your future once rested in the palms of my hands

Do I ever haunt you

The way you haunt me

I pray your robbing of innocence came to an end

I pray you didn't abuse the forgiveness I chose to extend

You were the chains

You were the stain

You were the reason I threw myself away

I keep trying to forget

But I guess I haven't forgiven myself yet

When things are good with him

I can smile

I can laugh

I can put all the bad into the depths

But when he opens my scars

Pours salt onto my bleeding heart

It all comes flooding back as if I never left

My soul is unable to find rest

So here I sit
Wine in hand

Waiting for the sun to rise again

For when it does

I'll begin to paint the smile across my face

The one that I pretend was never erased

Forgiving Me

I had lost so much hope in Martin and I finding peace together, so much so that it disrupted the peace I thought I had with my past. I realized that because of how lost I felt in my marriage, I was still hanging onto all of this self-loathing from everything before. I felt like I had made a huge mistake and married someone who didn't really love me, and that ripped my scars open deeper than I can put into words.

At this point, my dreams of bringing children into the world with this man had come true, but sadly my hatred for myself grew deeper than ever before in light of how much we weren't aligned as parents or as a couple. It had been my dream for so long, but like everything else, it felt tainted with a familiar darkness and loneliness. I knew in my heart that I couldn't change anything in my past and still have my children, but at the same time, I desperately longed for a chance to go back to January of 2013 and do everything differently. I wanted to go back in time and fight for myself and make better choices so they could have a father who truly loved their mother and them enough to stop running from his pain.

I wanted a man who would put God first and us second. Alcohol always seemed to hold both placeholders on the bad days; it felt like my husband's mistress. The lying about it, the anger at me for trying to control it, and the ugly haste he'd throw at me when

I'd call him out on what a different person it was turning him into…it was all too much for me to take on top of everything else. I had stood by him through thick and thin, even when he chose to leave me over alcohol or for friends who would offer up a seat and a drink. He would rather talk to strangers than me at times; if they had a drink in their hand, my heart in mine didn't seem to matter.

I always feared who he'd choose because I knew from past experiences that he was more than capable of leaving me when I needed him most. And that ate me alive. There were always good days mixed in with all of the bad, of course, but the bad ones haunted the good ones; they kept me awake at night, wondering when the other shoe was going to drop.

He was still the kindest, most hard-working person, and I cherished his heart. We pretty much never went to sleep without holding hands and that always made our love feel stronger than all the toxic things. But I still struggled with the hurt that followed when he'd cross the line with alcohol. He wasn't a mean drunk, but he'd just sort of disappear into an abyss. His touch still felt like home…I just didn't always feel like I could trust it to be a stable one.

During all the difficult days, I couldn't help but ask myself how I ended up here. But the truth was, I knew the answer. I had done the same thing that my husband was doing when we met; I was still running from everything, even if I didn't realize it. I thought that forgiving Charlie was my biggest obstacle, but ultimately, the greatest battle I had to face was *forgiving myself*. I didn't love myself enough to call things what they were in many areas of my life, not just with Charlie. I had grown so numb; it was like I was still stuck in a gear. Anytime something bad happened, I always covered it up with a smile or clung to whatever escape I could find in those moments. I wasn't putting God first. And I certainly wasn't making any room in my life to hear His whisper in the storms that I was in.

By some miracle, I finally began to *look up* again, and then everything eventually changed for the better. It had to start within the depths of me, but the peace that I prayed for found me right where I was at. I found healing within my heart because I realized my value for the first time in nearly a decade. And I think the reason things grew better for Martin and I was because he realized his value too. We looked up and saw that all the messes we'd both been through didn't define us in God's eyes. We rediscovered how much God loved us and how much we still loved each other. And it was beautiful.

A million awful fights later, it finally seemed like there was a light at the end of the tunnel. Ugly words that were said between us left scars, but the more that we began to turn to Jesus's scars, the more we found hope that all things could be made new. We saw what truly mattered in the light of His truth rather than the world's standards. It opened our eyes to so many good things that we'd been missing right in front of us all along. More than ever, we appreciated my parents; they had stood by us when we were at our worst, many times. They always showed up with tough love, but mostly just love. And that reflected God's grace and love for us when we needed to remember that most, both past and present.

We also had to part with some of the toxic friendships that didn't value our marriage or our family. Misery loves company held true for a lot of people that we once called friends. Sometimes people really don't want you to aim higher, and they spare no judgement when you choose to do better for yourself and the people that *really do love you*. We also had some friendships that vacated our life simply because the friendship never held any real depth; we learned who cared and who didn't. That was a bitter pill to swallow, but one that was necessary when we reached those crossroads. We came to find that *letting go* could be a very revealing and freeing thing.

At the end of the day, *nothing* and *no one* is perfect. My husband and I have a messy story, but it's a *real* story. It's a story about true friendship and our love surviving every bit of turbulence life threw our way. But most of all, it's a story that reflects God's love for us even when we were far from okay. I cherish what we have more than ever because I see His fingerprints so vibrantly present throughout our life song.

I thought I needed to put all of our mistakes into a pretty little box for me to live with them, but the truth is, I'm grateful for them. They are mile markers of lessons learned and reminders that we are so much more than our dark days or our regrets. And Lord knows we are never done making mistakes and screwing up in this life. He doesn't promise a life free from trials and pain, but He does promise to hold us through it all if we let Him.

I've never known anyone to be more forgiving, and more selfless at heart than Martin. It's something special that comes from within the depths of him as the roots of those characteristics certainly weren't taught or nurtured. His ability to persevere through trials and hurt has inspired me throughout the years I've been with him, and now more than ever that he's free of his old chains. The way he loves me has brought so much healing to the past, and the truth is, I always knew he loved me. Martin just struggled to love himself as I understood all too well. We all underestimate what it means to love ourselves, especially in the era that we live in.

When I look at pictures of us from our beginning, I think of all of the chaos we've survived together, and I smile. And I remember how our friendship prevailed through the thickest of storms because ultimately 'this thing'…this relationship that looked so bad on paper…it was the *real deal*. We never needed to prove anything to anyone, only to ourselves. Martin taught me that.

Marriage is hard. Having kids is hard. Life is just hard in general, even under the best of circumstances. We all have a past, and how we carry it affects not only us but everyone around us. Especially those who love us. I am grateful more than I can put into words for the way that my family chose to love me through my storms, and for the way they loved Martin through his. While I wish I hadn't let my past be such a destructive force on so much good I had been blessed with, I feel like because of God's grace, He was able to make something beautiful out of all that was broken.

Learning to love yourself is already a difficult thing to do in a world where everything around you is telling you you're not enough. That's all the more reason why it's so important to live by Audience of One and to put good things into your soul. You can't hear the Voice of Truth if you're only listening to the hundreds of other voices screaming and shouting lies at you. I didn't realize it back then, but I was fueling those voices all the time with the toxic stuff I was surrounding myself with. It felt so good to finally take a knife to the puppet strings the devil once had me strung up on. I had no idea that I had that power all along.

I don't regret forgiving. Forgiving Charlie. Forgiving people in my life that hurt me. And most of all, I don't regret loving them. *All of them*. Every relationship, even if it didn't last, was meaningful and special to me at one point or another. It got me through another day. My mother said it best when she always reminded me that people are for a reason, a season, or for life. I struggled with letting go of a lot of things, but eventually, I did learn to cling to the good. And while I wish I had learned to forgive myself sooner than I did, I might not have ever met my husband if I had. I don't think my heart would have ever been open to someone with his past had it not been for mine. I might not have ever had my precious children or the gift of being a bonus mom.

My stepson may never have had such loving and involved grandparents or a home like the one we ultimately made when his father and I began to put God first. Most of all, he may never have chosen to give his heart to Jesus. All of these things were a part of God's plans for me. He took the ugliness that the world cast onto me and turned it into something special and meaningful when I let Him. That's why I will always be grateful for this broken road that led me here…my beautiful mess where I finally reunited with every piece of me that I thought was lost forever.

The Beautiful Now

The scar may still remain, but I am no longer a slave to it. It does *not define me*. As I said at the beginning, this is not a story unlike many others out there, which is all the more reason why I felt compelled to share it. The stigma attached to the truth is often too heavy for us to bear with all the weight we are already carrying. The judgment and the blame often end up cast onto the wrong person when the truth comes to light. I pray that wherever you are in your story, you *look up*. Once you do, you'll slowly be able to regain peace because you'll reunite with The One who loves you unconditionally.

The stranger you become to survive the war within can sometimes end up being your worst enemy. You can wind up so callused that you forget the most important truths…that *you are valuable*. You are *loved*. You are *wanted*. And you have a purpose that can't be broken or taken away no matter what this world throws at you. It's so easy to lose sight of that in the darkest of days, but you are a daughter or son of The King. And I have news for the devil that he already knows deep down…Jesus wins. He's just trying to take as many of us down with him as he can before his time is up. *Don't let him.*

Whether you're in the trenches filled with anguish, no longer able to recognize yourself, or you're in such a numb place that you're just watching your dreams and your life fall apart on auto pilot, it's important to not judge yourself and to never lose hope. Unraveling doesn't always look like what you'd expect, and survival is never a straight line. All of us react differently to trauma. The brain does some pretty incredible things to try and protect itself from events that might be too overwhelming to accept. Sometimes, the swerves and zig zags are what keep us alive. But no matter what our journey has been, we are never too damaged for healing. We are never too messed up to be fixed. And we are never too far gone to be loved.

My story no longer collects dust in the back of my mind due to shame. While it wasn't an easy thing to share, if it were to help even just one person not feel alone in their pain, it was worth telling. I had never written this out before, probably because I felt like it would be too hard to relive my roller coaster, but it actually gave me more clarity. It helped me to see that I wasn't crazy…I was just learning to *survive* crazy.

I made a lot of bad choices, trusted the wrong people, gave grace to a fault, and drank too much, but in my reflection, I was reminded of *God's grace* and *His presence*. He showed up at every wrong turn with me and carried me through, even when I didn't know it. God really does make all things new when we release our broken hearts to Him. He can use the darkest parts of our stories to shine the brightest lights in this world…the devil hates that and tries to convince us otherwise. Against all odds, I pray you learn to breathe in all of the truths and exhale all the lies.

Most of all, I pray you let God's love be your safe haven; it is there that you will find pure solace and healing. It is there where you will see yourself through His eyes. And if you don't believe in God, that's okay…*He believes in you.*

NINETEEN UNSAID

Here's a list of some of the songs that really met me where I was at over the years. If you decide to listen to any of them, I hope the lyrics do the same for you.

Rescue-Lauren Daigle

Hold On To Me-Lauren Daigle

Wanted-Danny Gokey

Tell Your Heart to Beat Again-Danny Gokey

Whispers in the Dark-Skillet

Those Nights-Skillet

Broken-Lindsey Haun

Haunted-Maty Noyes

Never Alone-BarlowGirl

Answer-Sarah McLachlan

How Far-Tasha Layton

Never-Tasha Layton

Grateful-Rita Ora

Stand in the Rain-Superchick

Audience of One-Big Daddy Weave

New Creation-Mac Powell

Broken Hallelujah-The Afters

God Only Knows-for KING & COUNTRY

Not Alone-Red

Hold You Tight-Dan Bremnes

Innocent-Taylor Swift

Bird Set Free-Sia

Learning to Breathe-Switchfoot

Dare You to Move-Switchfoot

Find Me Tonight-Everyday Sunday

My Jesus-Anne Wilson

Me On Your Mind-Matthew West and Anne Wilson

My Story Your Glory-Matthew West

You Know Where to Find Me-Matthew West

Roses-Andrew Ripp

The Lost Get Found-Britt Nicole

The Sun is Rising-Britt Nicole

9 798330 375240